"*Costs of Sprawl* is a data-rich, amazingly robust yet pithy, highly readable account of sprawl's many impacts. Readers discover that living in a compact neighbourhood can add three years to your life, make it easier to own a home, and even spur upward mobility. It's a must-read for urban planners or anyone who cares about healthy, happy living."

Robert Cervero, Professor Emeritus,
Department of City & Regional Planning, University of California, Berkeley, USA;
Director, University of California Transportation Center, USA

Costs of Sprawl

Across the nation, the debate over metropolitan sprawl and its impact has become pivotal to urban planning. A decade and a half ago, Smart Growth America and the U.S. Environmental Protection Agency sought to raise the level of the debate by sponsoring groundbreaking research to quantitatively measure sprawl and its quality-of-life impacts. The resulting measures are widely used in urban research and public health.

Costs of Sprawl provides a panoramic guide to urban form in America, measures sprawl for metropolitan areas, urbanized areas, and counties, and studies the relationship between sprawl and quality-of-life outcomes. From this preliminary investigation, it looks like the costs of sprawl are varied and substantial, and the alternative of compact development is far superior.

An essential read for researchers, planners, urban designers, policy makers, and smart growth advocates in the U.S. and abroad, this book provides a comprehensive and detailed analysis of one of the most critical issues in planning today.

Reid Ewing, Ph.D., is a Professor of City and Metropolitan Planning at the University of Utah, USA, chair of the Department of City and Metropolitan Planning, associate editor of the *Journal of the American Planning Association*, columnist for *Planning* magazine, and one of the most highly cited academic planners in North America.

Shima Hamidi, Ph.D., is Director of the Institute of Urban Studies and Assistant Professor of Urban Planning. Hamidi is a transportation planner and a smart growth advocate. The results of her research have been cited in more than 100 national newspapers and magazines such as *Wall Street Journal, Washington Post* and *CNN Money*.

Costs of Sprawl

Reid Ewing and Shima Hamidi

Routledge
Taylor & Francis Group
NEW YORK AND LONDON

First published 2017
by Routledge
711 Third Avenue, New York, NY 10017

and by Routledge
2 Park Square, Milton Park, Abingdon, Oxon, OX14 4RN

Routledge is an imprint of the Taylor & Francis Group, an informa business

© 2017 Taylor & Francis

The right of Reid Ewing and Shima Hamidi to be identified as authors of this work
has been asserted by him/her/them in accordance with sections 77 and 78 of the
Copyright, Designs and Patents Act 1988.

All rights reserved. No part of this book may be reprinted or reproduced or utilised
in any form or by any electronic, mechanical, or other means, now known or hereafter
invented, including photocopying and recording, or in any information storage or
retrieval system, without permission in writing from the publishers.

Trademark notice: Product or corporate names may be trademarks or registered
trademarks, and are used only for identification and explanation without intent
to infringe.

Library of Congress Cataloging-in-Publication Data
Names: Ewing, Reid H., author. | Hamidi, Shima, author.
Title: Costs of sprawl / Reid Ewing and Shima Hamidi.
Description: 1 Edition. | New York : Routledge, 2017. | Includes index.
Identifiers: LCCN 2016057635 | ISBN 978-1-138-64551-6 (pbk.)
| ISBN 978-1-315-62810-3 (ebook)
Subjects: LCSH: Cities and towns—United States—Growth.
Classification: LCC HT384.U5 .E95 2017 | DDC 307.1/4160973—dc23LC
record available at https://lccn.loc.gov/2016057635

ISBN: 978-1-138-08136-9 (hbk)
ISBN: 978-1-138-64551-6 (pbk)
ISBN: 978-1-315-62810-3 (ebk)

Typeset in Bembo and Trade Gothic
by Fish Books Ltd.

Contents

	List of Figures and Tables	viii
	Acknowledgements	xiii
1	Introduction	1
2	Updated County Sprawl Index	14
3	Refined County Sprawl Measures	22
4	Validation of County Sprawl Indices	41
5	Traffic Safety	56
6	Public Health	71
7	Derivation and Validation of Metropolitan Sprawl Indices	89
8	Relationship of Sprawl to Topical Outcomes	109
9	Urbanized Areas: A Longitudinal Analysis	143
10	Case Examples for Planners	159
	Index	166

List of Figures and Tables

Figures

1.1	Aerial Images of Portland and Raleigh at the Same Scale	7
2.1	Scatterplot of 2010 Sprawl Index vs. 2000 Sprawl Index (Estimated Equivalently)	20
2.2	Histogram of Changes in County Sprawl Index Between 2000 and 2010 (Estimated Equivalently)	21
3.1	Most Compact County According to Both Indices (New York County, NY)	32
3.2	Second Most Compact County According to Both Indices (Kings County, NY)	33
3.3	Most Sprawling County According to Six-Variable Index (Jackson County, KS)	34
3.4	Second Most Sprawling County According to Six-Variable Index (Polk County, MN)	35
3.5	Most Sprawling County According to Four-Factor Index (Oglethorpe County, GA)	35
3.6	Second Most Sprawling County According to Four-Factor Index (Grant Parish, LA)	37
4.1	Frequency Distribution of the Percentage of Commute Walk Trips by County	44
4.2	Frequency Distribution of the Natural Logarithm of the Percentage of Commute Walk Trips by County	45
4.3	Scatterplot of Natural Logarithm of the Commute Walk Mode Share vs. the Original Compactness Index	46

List of Figures and Tables

4.4	Scatterplot of Natural Logarithm of the Commute Walk Mode Share vs. the Natural Logarithm of Original Compactness Index	47
5.1	Causal Path Diagram for Fatal Crashes in Terms of County Compactness, VMT, and Other Variables	63
7.1	Most Compact Metropolitan Areas (New York and San Francisco)	99
7.2	Most Sprawling Metropolitan Areas (Atlanta and Hickory, NC)	100
7.3	Central Business District and Employment Subcenters in Washington DC Metropolitan Division	104
7.4	Detroit 2010 Metropolitan Division (dark) versus Detroit 2000 PMSA Boundary (light)	105
7.5	Portland Metropolitan Area Boundary in 2010 versus. Portland PMSA Boundary in 2000	106
8.1	Causal Path Diagram for Life Expectancy in Terms of County Compactness and Other Variables	115
8.2	Causal Path Diagram for Upward Mobility in Terms of Metropolitan/Commuting Zone Compactness and Other Variables	133

Tables

1.1	Variable Loadings on the Census Tract Compactness Index for 2010	8
2.1	County Sprawl Index Variables and Factor Loadings in 2010	18
2.2	10 Most Compact Counties in 2010 According to the Six Variable Index	19
2.3	10 Most Sprawling Counties in 2010 According to the Six Variable Index	19
3.1	Variable Loadings on the County Density Factor for 2010	24
3.2	Variable Loadings on the County Mix Factor for 2010	25
3.3	Variable Loadings on the County Centering Factor for 2010	27
3.4	Variable Loadings on the County Street Factor for 2010	28
3.5	Simple Pearson Correlation Between Four Factors	29
3.6	10 Most Compact Counties in 2010 According to the Four-Factor Index (excluding Massachusetts counties)	30
3.7	10 Most Sprawling Counties in 2010 According to the Four-Factor Index (excluding Massachusetts counties)	31
3.8	10 Most Sprawling Counties in 2010 According to the Six-Variable Index	34

List of Figures and Tables

3.9	10 Most Sprawling Counties in 2010 According to the Four-Factor Index (excluding Massachusetts counties)	35
4.1	Variables Used to Explain Travel Outcomes (all variables log transformed)	43
4.2	Relationships to Average Household Vehicle Ownership (log-log form with robust standard errors)	48
4.3	Relationships to Walk Mode Share (log-log form with robust standard errors)	50
4.4	Relationships to Transit Mode Share (log-log form with robust standard errors)	52
4.5	Relationships to Average Drive Time (log-log form with robust standard errors)	54
5.1	Crash Database	58
5.2	Variables (variables log transformed)	60
5.3	Direct Effects of Variables on One Another in the Fatal Crash Model (log-log form)	64
5.4	Direct, Indirect, and Total Effects of the Original Compactness Index and Other Variables on the Fatal Crash Rate	65
5.5	Direct, Indirect, and Total Effects of the New Compactness Index and Other Variables on the Fatal Crash Rate	65
5.6	Direct Effects of Variables on One Another in the Total Crash Model (log-log form)	66
5.7	Direct, Indirect, and Total Effects of the Original Compactness Index and Other Variables on the Total Crash Rate	66
5.8	Direct, Indirect, and Total Effects of the New Compactness Index and Other Variables on the Total Crash Rate	67
5.9	Direct Effects of Variables on One Another in the Non-fatal Injury Crash Model (log-log form)	67
5.10	Direct, Indirect, and Total Effects of the Original Compactness Index and Other Variables on the Non-fatal Injury Crash Rate	68
5.11	Direct, Indirect, and Total Effects of the New Compactness Index and Other Variables on the Non-fatal Injury Crash Rate	68
6.1	BRFSS Variables and Sample Sizes	76
6.2	Relationships to BMI (with robust standard errors)	79
6.3	Relationships to Obesity (with robust standard errors)	80
6.4	Relationships to Any Physical Activity (with robust standard errors)	81
6.5	Relationships to Minutes of Moderate Physical Activity per Week (with robust standard errors)	82

List of Figures and Tables

6.6.	Relationships to High Blood Pressure (with robust standard errors) 82	
6.7	Relationships to Coronary Heart Disease (with robust standard errors)	83
6.8	Relationships to Diabetes (with robust standard errors)	83
7.1	Variable Loadings of Four Factors for 2010	95
7.2	Compactness/Sprawl Scores for 10 Most Compact and 10 Most Sprawling Metropolitan Areas and Divisions in 2010	98
7.3	Variables Used to Explain Transportation Outcomes (all variables log transformed)	101
7.4	Relationships of the Overall Indices to Transportation Outcomes (log–log transformed – t-statistics in parentheses)	102
7.5	Relationships of Individual Compactness Factors to Transportation Outcomes (log–log transformed – t-statistics in parentheses)	103
8.1	County Variables (variables log transformed)	114
8.2	Direct Effects of Variables on One Another in the Life Expectancy Model	116
8.3	Direct, Indirect, and Total Effects of the County level Sprawl Index and Other Variables on Life Expectancy	117
8.4	Variables Used to Explain Housing + Transportation Affordability (variables log transformed)	121
8.5	Relationships to Housing Affordability (log–log form with robust standard errors)	122
8.6	Relationships to Transportation Affordability (log–log form with robust standard errors)	123
8.7	Relationships to Housing + Transportation Affordability (log–log form with robust standard errors)	124
8.8	Variables Used to Explain Upward Mobility	131
8.9	Direct Effects of Variables on One Another in the Upward Mobility Model	134
8.10	Direct, Indirect, and Total Effects of the Metropolitan Compactness Index and Other Variables on Upward Mobility	135
9.1	Variable Loadings on Four Factors for 2010	149
9.2	Compactness/Sprawl Scores for 10 Most Compact and 10 Most Sprawling UZAs in 2010	151
9.3	Compactness/Sprawl Scores for 10 Most Compact and 10 Most Sprawling UZAs in 2000	152
9.4	Variables Used to Explain Travel Outcomes (all variables log transformed)	153

List of Figures and Tables

9.5   Relationships of UZA Compactness Index in 2010 to
       Transportation Outcomes (log–log transformed – t-statistics
       in parentheses)   154
9.6   Relationships of 2010 UZA Individual Compactness Factors
       to Transportation Outcomes (log–log transformed – t-statistics
       in parentheses)   155

Acknowledgements

This research was funded by the National Institutes of Health, the Ford Foundation, and Smart Growth America. The authors wish to thank David Berrigan, Don Chen, and Geoff Anderson, respectively.

Chapter One

Introduction

Across the nation, the debate over metropolitan sprawl and its impact continues decade after decade. There is little agreement on the definition of sprawl or its alternatives: compact development, pedestrian-friendly design, transit-oriented development, and the catch-all term "smart growth." There is also little consensus about how sprawl impacts everything from housing affordability and traffic congestion to open space preservation and air quality (Burchell et al. 1998, 2002; Bruegmann 2006; Duany et al. 2001; Ewing 1997; Ewing et al. 2002; Gordon and Richardson 1997; Hayden 2004; Hirschhorn 2005; Kahn 2006a). Duany et al. (2001) use cultural, aesthetic, and ecological reasons to reject suburban sprawl as human habitat. At the other end of the spectrum, Bruegmann (2006) describes suburban sprawl as a natural manifestation of the American Dream of a big house in the suburbs.

A decade ago, Smart Growth America (SGA) and the U.S. Environmental Protection Agency (EPA) sought to raise the level of this debate by sponsoring groundbreaking research on sprawl and its quality-of-life consequences (Ewing et al. 2002. 2003a, 2003b, 2003c). The original sprawl indices were made available to researchers who wished to explore the various costs and benefits of sprawl. They have been widely used in outcome-related research, particularly in connection with public health. Sprawl has been linked to physical inactivity, obesity, traffic fatalities, poor air quality, residential energy use, emergency response times, teenage driving, lack of social capital, and private-vehicle commute distances and times (Bereitschaft and Debbage 2013; Cho et al. 2006; Doyle et al. 2006; Ewing et al. 2003a, 2003b, 2003c, 2006; Ewing and Rong 2008; Fan and Song 2009; Griffin et al. 2013; Holcombe and Williams 2012; Joshu et al. 2008; Kahn 2006a; Kelly-Schwartz et al. 2004; Kim et al. 2006; Kostova 2011; Lee et al. 2009; McDonald and Trowbridge 2009; Nguyen 2010;

1

Introduction

Plantinga and Bernell 2007; Schweitzer and Zhou 2010; Stone 2008; Stone et al. 2010; Sturm and Cohen 2004; Trowbridge and McDonald 2008; Trowbridge et al. 2009; Zolnik 2011).

In this study for the National Cancer Institute, the Ford Foundation, and SGA, we update the original sprawl indices to 2010. Additionally, we develop refined versions of the indices that incorporate more measures of the built environment. Finally, we validate these indices against U.S. American Community Survey (ACS) data for journey to work, Fatality Analysis Reporting System (FARS) data on traffic fatality and pedestrian fatality rates, and Behavioral Risk Factor Surveillance System (BRFSS) data on overweight and obesity. It is our hope that the updated and refined sprawl measures developed and validated in this book will find as widespread use in the fields of urban planning and public health as have the original indices.

Urban Sprawl Generally

Urban sprawl (also referred to as suburban sprawl) has become the dominant metropolitan development pattern in the U.S. Examples of compact development, the antithesis of sprawl, are so few and far between that they seem almost quaint these days. For every New York metropolitan area, there are dozens of Atlantas. For every Manhattan, there are hundreds of Walton counties (county located on the periphery of the Atlanta metropolitan).

As the costs of sprawl have become more apparent, the term urban sprawl has gone from urban planning construct to public policy concern. But what exactly is urban sprawl? In the early 1990s, one of the authors of this book worked on a definition of sprawl for purposes of growth management in Florida. The definition ultimately adopted by the State encompassed the following urban forms: (1) leapfrog or scattered development, (2) commercial strip development, (3) expanses of low-density development, or (4) expanses of single-use development (as in sprawling bedroom communities). Because these forms are prototypical, and a matter of degree, the Florida definition was supplemented with "primary indicators" of sprawl that could be measured and made subject to regulation. The most important indicator, which became part of the law, was any development pattern characterized by poor accessibility among related land uses.

All four prototypical patterns (leapfrog, etc.) are characterized by poor accessibility (Ewing 1997). In scattered or leapfrog development, residents and service providers must pass vacant land on their way from one developed use to another. In classic strip development, the consumer must pass other uses on the way from

Introduction

one store to the next; it is the antithesis of multipurpose travel to an activity center. Of course, in low-density, single-use development, everything is far apart due to large private land holdings and segregation of land uses. The potential link to public policy is clear. In sprawl, poor accessibility of land uses to one another may leave residents with no alternative to miles and miles of automobile travel.

Early Attempts to Measure Sprawl

The first attempts to measure the extent of urban sprawl were crude. Several researchers created measures of urban sprawl that focused on density (Anthony 2004; Burchfield et al. 2006; Fulton et al. 2001; Lang 2003; Lopez and Hynes 2003; Malpezzi and Guo 2001; Nasser and Overberg 2001; Pendall 1999; Pendall and Carruthers 2003;). Pendall (1999) sought to explain the incidence of sprawl for large metropolitan areas in terms of land values, metropolitan political organization, local government spending, traffic congestion, and various local land use policies. Pendall's measure of sprawl was strictly related to density. Population was divided by urban acreage to obtain density estimates for 1982 and 1992, with urban acreage taken from the U.S. Department of Agriculture's National Resources Inventory. To measure increases in sprawl over time, estimates of population change between 1982 and 1992 were divided by estimates of change in urban land during the same period. By this measure, Los Angeles, San Francisco, and San Diego were the most compact metros in 1992, while Milwaukee, Atlanta, Cleveland, and Denver were the most sprawling. Baltimore, Los Angeles, and San Diego grew in the most compact manner over the decade, while Boston, Cincinnati, and Minneapolis-St. Paul grew in the least.

Building on Pendall's earlier work, Fulton et al. (2001) studied urban land consumption relative to population change for every U.S. metropolitan area. If land is consumed at a faster rate than population is growing, sprawl is said to be increasing. As with Pendall's earlier work, this concept of sprawl is strictly density-related. By this criterion, the West is home to some of the least sprawling metropolitan areas in the nation. By contrast, the Northeast and Midwest are in some ways the nation's biggest sprawl problems since they add few new residents, yet consume large amounts of land. In this study, Honolulu and Los Angeles were rated most compact in 1997, and Las Vegas and Phoenix (often characterized as sprawling badly) were both in the top 20 in compactness. Las Vegas and Phoenix were first and third in density gain over the 15 years studied (1982 to 1997).

The report by Fulton et al. (2001) also examined the causes of sprawl. Metropolitan areas tend to consume less land for urbanization—relative to

Introduction

population growth—when they are growing rapidly in population, rely heavily on public water and sewer systems, and have large immigrant populations. Metropolitan areas tend to consume more land for urbanization—again, relative to population growth—if they are compact to begin with and have fragmented local governance.

Taking a different tack, Glaeser et al. (2001) related sprawl to the degree of decentralization of employment using data from the U.S. Department of Commerce's Zip Code Business Patterns for 1996. Zip code business pattern data were extracted from the Standard Statistical Establishments List, a file of all single and multi-establishment companies listed by zip code and firm size.

For the 100 largest U.S. metropolitan areas, the share of overall metropolitan employment within a three-mile ring of the central business district (CBD) was computed, as were the shares inside and outside a 10-mile ring. The share within 3 miles reflects the presence or absence of a well-defined employment core, while the share beyond 10 miles captures the extent of job sprawl. Metros were then divided into four categories, based on values of these indices. Dense employment metros like New York have at least one quarter of their employ-ment within 3 miles of the city center. Centralized employment metros like Minneapolis–St. Paul have between 10 and 25 percent of employment within 3 miles of the city center, and more than 60 percent within 10 miles. Decentral-ized employment metros like Washington D.C. have 10 to 25 percent of employment within the 3-mile ring, and less than 60 percent within 10 miles. Finally, extremely decentralized employment metros like Los Angeles have less than 10 percent of their employment within the 3-mile ring. A follow-up study for the Brookings Institution used the same metrics to rate the degree of sprawl in metropolitan areas as of 2006 (Kneebone 2009).

The ease of measurement associated with the early sprawl indices came with a lack of precision that led to wildly different sprawl ratings given to different metropolitan areas by different analysts. In one study, Portland was listed as the most compact region and Los Angeles was ranked among the most sprawling. In another, their rankings were essentially reversed (Glaeser et al. 2001; Nasser and Overberg 2001). More importantly, such measures disregarded other qualities commonly associated with sprawl such as segregated land uses, commercial strips, and leapfrog development (Ewing 1997).

Recent Use of Satellite Imagery

The same mistakes made in early quantitative studies of sprawl (neglect of land use interactions and quality-of-life outcomes) have been made in recent studies

Introduction

using satellite imagery (Huang et al. 2007; Martellozzo and Clarke 2011). Huang et al. (2007), for instance, calculated seven spatial metrics that capture five distinct dimensions of urban form (complexity, centrality, compactness, porosity, and density) in order to compare different cities and countries throughout the world. Such methods are useful for comparing one metropolitan or urbanized area with another. However, these methods are limited in their ability to distinguish patterns of high accessibility from patterns of low accessibility because they ignore detailed land use and street patterns.

Multiple Dimensions

Most scholars now agree that sprawl is a multi-dimensional phenomenon (Cutsinger et al. 2005; Ewing et al. 2002; Frenkel and Ashkenazi 2008; Galster et al. 2001; Jaeger et al. 2010; Malpezzi and Guo 2001; Mubareka et al. 2011; Torrens 2008). But this can lead to more questions than answers. What are the dimensions of sprawl? How are they best measured? Should these dimensions be combined into an overall sprawl index and, if so, how? Is sprawl in all dimensions necessary to call an urban area "sprawling"? Are tradeoffs allowed?

The first multi-dimensional measures of sprawl were developed by Galster et al. (2001). They disaggregated land-use patterns into eight dimensions: density, continuity, concentration, clustering, centrality, nuclearity, heterogeneity (mixing), and proximity. Sprawl was defined as a pattern of land use that has low levels in one or more of these dimensions. The researchers operationally defined each dimension and successfully quantified 6 of the 8 measures for 13 urbanized areas. New York and Philadelphia ranked as the least sprawling of the 13, and Atlanta and Miami as the most sprawling.

Since then, Galster and his colleagues have extended their sprawl measures to more than 50 metropolitan areas, confirming the multi-dimensional nature of sprawl. In one study, they ranked metropolitan areas using 14 different dimensions, some related to population, others to employment, and still others to both (Cutsinger et al. 2005). The 14 dimensions, which were reduced to 7 factors through principal component analysis, however, tended to cancel out each other. Metropolitan areas ranking near the top on one factor were likely to rank near the bottom on another. Los Angeles, for example, ranked second on both "mixed use" and "housing centrality," but 48th on "proximity" and 49th on "nuclearity." With so many overlapping variables, the analysis became confused.

Ewing et al. (2002) also developed sprawl indices that, like Galster's, were multi-dimensional, but were more focused and demonstrated wider degrees of

Introduction

variability among metropolitan areas. They defined sprawl as any environment with: (1) a population widely dispersed in low-density residential development; (2) a rigid separation of homes, shops, and workplaces; (3) a lack of major employment and population concentrations downtown and in suburban town centers and other activity centers; and (4) a network of roads marked by very large block sizes and poor access from one place to another. The authors used these indices to measure sprawl for 83 of the nation's largest metropolitan areas, standardizing the indices with mean values of 100 and standard deviations of 25. The indices were constructed so that the more compact a metropolitan area was, the larger its index value. More sprawling metropolitan areas had smaller index values. Thus, in the year 2000, the relatively compact Portland, Oregon, metropolitan area had an index value of 126, while the slightly smaller Raleigh-Durham metropolitan area had an index value of 54 (Figure 1.1). Los Angeles ended up near the middle of the pack, with an index of 102.

Recap of Past Studies

The most notable feature of past studies (with few exceptions like that of Galster et al.) is the failure to define sprawl in all its complexity. Density is relatively easy to measure, and hence serves as the sole indicator of sprawl in several studies. This flies in the face of both the technical literature and popular conceptions of sprawl.

Another notable feature, related to the first, is the wildly different sprawl ratings given to different metros by different analysts. With the exception of Atlanta, which always seems to rank as one of the worst, the different variables used to operationalize sprawl lead to very different results. In one study, Portland is ranked as most compact and Los Angeles is way down the list. In another their rankings are essentially reversed. In a third study, certain Northeastern metros are characterized as sprawling; in a fourth they are relatively compact.

A third notable feature was the failure to validate sprawl measures vis-à-vis impacts such as automobile dependence. Related to this, earlier studies paid little attention to the impacts of sprawl generally. It is the impacts of sprawl that concern planners and public officials, not the patterns themselves. With the exception of a few studies focusing on individual impacts, the literature was nearly devoid of empiricism. Sprawl was presumed to have negative consequences, or presumed to be free of them, depending on the ideological bent of the author.

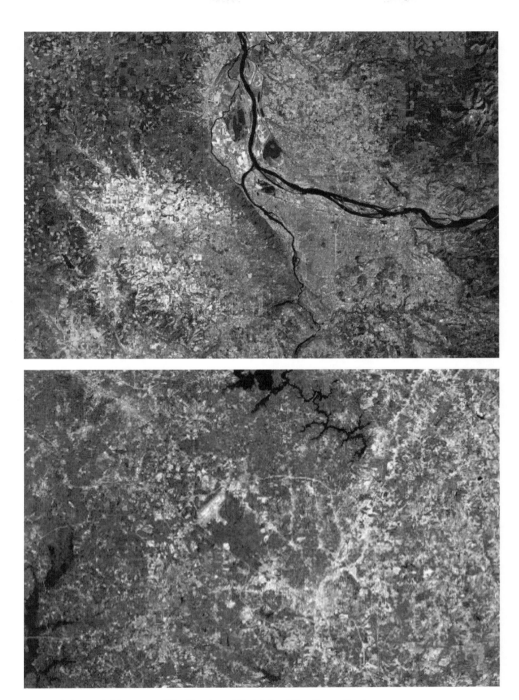

Figure 1.1: Aerial Images of Portland and Raleigh at the Same Scale
Source: www.maps.google.com

Introduction

Small Area Measures

The concept of sprawl naturally brings to mind large geographic areas. When we say Atlanta sprawls badly, we are referring to the Atlanta Metropolitan Area, or perhaps if we are a transportation planner, to the Atlanta Urbanized Area. From the earliest writings on sprawl, sprawl was said to occur primarily at the periphery of urbanized areas moving outward. An individual street or block may contribute to sprawl, but we would not say it is sprawl. This distinction seems particularly poignant when we talk about population and employment centering, which is defined by interrelationships among block groups. If one block group or a group of them has a significantly higher density than those surrounding it, we can say the former serves as a center for the block groups surrounding it.

Yet, we know from the travel and public health literatures that there is a demand from the research community for built environmental metrics at the sub-county level, what might be described as the community or neighborhood scale. Most of the built environment-travel studies, and most of the built environment-physical activity studies, have related individual outcomes to the built environment at a relatively small scale. Therefore, we have derived sprawl-like metrics for census tracts within metropolitan areas, and posted them along with metropolitan area, urbanized area, and county sprawl metrics on the

Table 1.1: Variable Loadings on the Census Tract Compactness Index for 2010

Component Matrix		Data Sources	Factor Loadings
Density Factor			
popden	gross population density	Census 2010	0.666
empden	gross employment density	LED 2010	0.298
jobpop	job–population balance	LED 2010	0.486
jobmix	degree of job mixing (entropy)	LED 2010	0.664
walkscore	weighted average Walk Score	Walk Score Inc.	0.821
smlblk	percentage of small urban blocks	Census 2010	0.677
avgblksze	average block size	Census 2010	−0.787
intden	intersection density	TomTom 2007	0.841
4way	percentage of four-or-more-way intersections	TomTom 2007	0.621
Eigenvalue			4.27
Explained variance			42.7%

National Institutes of Health (NIH) website (http://gis.cancer.gov/tools/urban-sprawl/).

We have used the same type of variables as in larger area analyses, extracted principal components from multiple variables using principal component analysis, and once again, transformed the first principal component to an index with the mean of 100 and a standard deviation of 25. The component variables are listed in Table 1.1. Because the number of component variables is greater for street accessibility than land-use mix, and greater for land-use mix than development density, the resulting index gives more weight to street accessibility than mix, and to mix than density. This is not unintentional, since the built environment-travel literature suggests that density is the least important of the three D variable types (Ewing and Cervero 2010).

References

Anthony, J. (2004). Do state growth management regulations reduce sprawl? *Urban Affairs Review*, 39(3), 376–397.

Bereitschaft, B., and Debbage, K. (2013). Urban form, air pollution, and CO_2 emissions in large U.S. metropolitan areas. *The Professional Geographer*, 65(4), 612–635.

Bruegmann, R. (2006). *Sprawl: A compact history*. University of Chicago Press, Chicago, IL.

Burchell, R.W., Shad, N.A., Listokin, D., Phillips, H., Seskin, S., Davis, J.S., Moore, T., Helton, D., and Gall, M. (1998). *The Costs of Sprawl-Revisited*. Transportation Research Board Report 39, National Academy Press, Washington, D.C.

Burchell, R.W., Lowenstein, G., Dolphin, W.R., Galley, C.C., Downs, A., Seskin, S., Gray Still, K., and Moore, T. (2002). *Costs of Sprawl 2000*. TCRP Report 74, Transit Cooperative Research Program, Transportation Research Board, Washington, D.C.

Burchfield, M., Overman, H.G., Puga, D., and Turner, M. (2006). Causes of sprawl: A portrait from space. *Quarterly Journal of Economics*, 121(2), 587–633.

Cho, S., Chen, Z., Yen, S.T. and Eastwood, D.B. (2006). *The Effects of Urban Sprawl on Body Mass Index: Where People Live Does Matter*. The 52nd Annual ACCI Conference, Baltimore, Maryland, March 15–18.

Cutsinger, J., Galster, G., Wolman, H., Hanson, R., and Towns, D. (2005). Verifying the multi-dimensional nature of metropolitan land use: Advancing the understanding and measurement of sprawl. *Journal of Urban Affairs*, 27(3), 235–259.

Introduction

Doyle, S., Kelly-Schwartz, A., Schlossberg, M., and Stockard, J. (2006). Active community environments and health: The relationship of walkable and safe communities to individual health. *Journal of the American Planning Association*, 72(1), 19–31.

Duany, A., Plater-Zyberk, E., and Speck, J. (2001). *Suburban Nation: The rise of sprawl and the decline of the American dream*. North Point Press, New York.

Ewing, R. (1997). Is Los Angeles-style sprawl desirable? *Journal of the American Planning Association*, 63(1), 107–126.

Ewing, R., and Cervero, R. (2010). Travel and the built environment: A meta-analysis. *Journal of the American Planning Association*, 76(3), 265–294.

Ewing, R., and Rong, F. (2008). Impact of urban form on U.S. residential energy use. *Housing Policy Debate*, 19, 1–30.

Ewing, R., Pendall, R., and Chen, D. (2002). *Measuring Sprawl and its Impacts*. Smart Growth America, Washington, D.C.

Ewing, R., Pendall, R., and Chen, D. (2003a). Measuring sprawl and its transportation impacts. *Transportation Research Record*, 1832, 175–183.

Ewing R., Schmid, T., Killingsworth, R., Zlot, A., and Raudenbush, S. (2003b). Relationship between urban sprawl and physical activity, obesity, and morbidity. *American Journal of Health Promotion*, 18, 47–57.

Ewing, R., Schieber, R., and Zegeer, C. (2003c). Urban sprawl as a risk factor in motor vehicle occupant and pedestrian fatalities. *American Journal of Public Health*, 93, 1541–1545.

Ewing R., Brownson, R., and Berrigan, D. (2006). Relationship between urban sprawl and weight of U.S. youth. *American Journal of Preventive Medicine*, 31, 464–474.

Fan, Y., and Song, Y. (2009). Is sprawl associated with a widening urban–suburban mortality gap? *Journal of Urban Health: Bulletin of the New York Academy of Medicine*, 86(5), 708–728.

Frenkel, A., and Ashkenazi, M. (2008). Measuring urban sprawl: How can we deal with it? *Environment and Planning B: Planning and Design*, 35(1), 56–79.

Fulton, W., Pendall, R., Nguyen, M., and Harrison, A. (2001). *Who Sprawls Most? How Growth Patterns Differ Across the U.S.*, Center for Urban & Metropolitan Policy, The Brookings Institution, Washington, D.C.

Galster, G., Hanson, R., Ratcliffe, M.R., Wolman, H., Coleman, S., and Freihage, J. (2001). Wrestling sprawl to the ground: Defining and measuring an elusive concept. *Housing policy debate,* 12(4), 681–717.

Glaeser, E., Kahn, M., and Chu, C. (2001). *Job Sprawl: Employment Location in U.S. Metropolitan Areas, Center for Urban & Metropolitan Policy*, The Brookings Institution, Washington, D.C.

Gordon, P., and Richardson, H.W. (1997). Are compact cities a desirable planning goal? *Journal of the American Planning Association*, 63(1), 95–106.

Griffin, B.A., Eibner, C., Bird, C.E., Jewell, A., Margolis, K., Shih, R., and Escarce, J.J. (2013). The relationship between urban sprawl and coronary heart disease in women. *Health & Place*, 20, 51–61.

Hayden, D. (2004). *A Field Guide to Sprawl*, W.W. Norton & Company, New York.

Hirschhorn, J.S. (2005). *Sprawl Kills: How bland burbs steal your time, health and money*, Sterling & Ross, New York.

Holcombe, R.G., and Williams, D.W. (2012). Urban sprawl and transportation externalities. *The Review of Regional Studies*, 40(3), 257–272.

Huang, J., Lu, X.X., and Sellers, J.M. (2007). A global comparative analysis of urban form: Applying spatial metrics and remote sensing. *Landscape and Urban Planning*, 82(4), 184–197.

Jaeger, J.A., Bertiller, R., Schwick, C., and Kienast, F. (2010). Suitability criteria for measures of urban sprawl. *Ecological Indicators*, 10(2), 397–406.

Joshu, C.E., Boehmer, T.K., Brownson, R.C., and Ewing, R. (2008). Personal, neighbourhood and urban factors associated with obesity in the United States. *Journal of Epidemiology and Community Health*, 62, 202–208.

Kahn, M.E. (2006a). *The Quality of Life in Sprawled Versus Compact Cities*, prepared for the OECD ECMT Regional Round, Berkeley, California, March 2006, Table 137, 27–28.

Kahn, M.E. (2006b). *Green Cities: Urban growth and the environment*. Brookings Institution Press, Washington, D.C.

Kelly-Schwartz, A., Stockard, J., Doyle, S., and Schlossberg, M. (2004). Is sprawl unhealthy? A multilevel analysis of the relationship of metropolitan sprawl to the health of individuals. *Journal of Planning Education and Research*, 24, 184–196.

Kim, D., Subramanian, S.V., Gortmaker, S.L., and Kawachi, I. (2006). U.S. state- and county-level social capital in relation to obesity and physical inactivity: A multilevel, multivariable analysis. *Social Science & Medicine*, 63(4), 1045–1059.

Kneebone, E. (2009). *Job Sprawl Revisited: The Changing Geography of Metropolitan Employment*, Metro Economy Series for the Metropolitan Policy Program at Brookings, Brookings Institution Press, Washington D.C.

Kostova, D. (2011). Can the built environment reduce obesity? The impact of residential sprawl and neighborhood parks on obesity and physical activity. *Eastern Economic Journal*, 37(3), 390–402.

Lang, R. (2003). *Edgeless Cities: Exploring the elusive metropolis*, Brookings Institution Press, Washington, D.C.

Introduction

Lee, I.M., Ewing, R., and Sesso, H.D. (2009). The built environment and physical activity levels: The Harvard Alumni Health Study. *American Journal of Preventive Medicine*, 37(4), 293–298.

Lopez, R., and Hynes, H.P. (2003). Sprawl in the 1990s: Measurement, distribution, and trends. *Urban Affairs Review*, 38(3), 325–355.

Malpezzi, S., and Guo, W.K. (2001). *Measuring 'Sprawl': Alternative Measures of Urban Form in U.S. Metropolitan Areas*, Center for Urban Land Economics Research, University of Wisconsin, Madison, WI.

Martellozzo, F., and Clarke, K.C. (2011). Measuring urban sprawl, coalescence, and dispersal: a case study of Pordenone, Italy. *Environment and Planning B: Planning and Design*, 38(6), 1085–1104.

McDonald, N., and Trowbridge, M. (2009). Does the built environment affect when American teens become drivers? Evidence from the 2001 National Household Travel Survey. *Journal of Safety Research*, 40(3), 177–183.

Mubareka, S., Koomen, E., Estreguil, C., and Lavalle, C. (2011). Development of a composite index of urban compactness for land use modelling applications. *Landscape and Urban Planning*, 103(3), 303–317.

Nasser, H., and Overberg, P. (2001). A comprehensive look at sprawl in America. *USA Today*, 22: 1.

Nguyen, D. (2010). Evidence of the impacts of urban sprawl on social capital. *Environment and Planning B: Planning and Design*, 37(4), 610–627.

Pendall, R. (1999). Do land-use controls cause sprawl? *Environment and Planning B*, 26(4), 555–571.

Pendall, R., and Carruthers, J.I. (2003). Does density exacerbate income segregation? Evidence from U.S. metropolitan areas, 1980 to 2000. *Housing Policy Debate*, 14(4), 541–589.

Plantinga, A., and Bernell, S. (2007). The association between urban sprawl and obesity: Is it a two-way street? *Journal of Regional Science*, 47(5), 857–879.

Schweitzer, L., and Zhou, J. (2010). Neighborhood air quality outcomes in compact and sprawled regions. *Journal of the American Planning Association*, 76(3), 363–371

Stone, B. (2008). Urban sprawl and air quality in large U.S. cities. *Journal of Environmental Management*, 86, 688–698.

Stone, B., Hess, J., and Frumkin, H. (2010). Urban form and extreme heat events: Are sprawling cities more vulnerable to climate change than compact cities? *Environmental Health Perspectives*, 118(10), 1425–1428.

Sturm, R., and Cohen, D. (2004). Suburban sprawl and physical and mental health. *Public Health*, 118(7), 488–496.

Torrens, P. (2008). A toolkit for measuring sprawl. *Applied Spatial Analysis and Policy*, 1(1), 5–36.

Trowbridge, M.J., and McDonald, N.C. (2008). Urban sprawl and miles driven daily by teenagers in the United States. *American Journal of Preventive Medicine*, 34(3), 202–206.

Trowbridge, M.J., Gurka, M.J., and O'Connor, R. (2009). Urban sprawl and delayed ambulance arrival in the United States. *American Journal of Preventive Medicine*, 37(5), 428–432.

Zolnik, E.J. (2011). The effect of sprawl on private-vehicle commuting outcomes. *Environment and Planning A*, 43(8), 1875–1893.

Chapter Two

Updated County Sprawl Index

Ewing et al. (2003b; 2003c) originally estimated a single county sprawl index for each of 448 metropolitan counties or statistically equivalent entities (e.g., independent towns and cities). These counties comprised the 101 most populous metropolitan statistical areas, consolidated metropolitan statistical areas, and New England county metropolitan areas in the U.S. as of the 1990 Census, the latest year for which metropolitan boundaries were defined as that study began. Nonmetropolitan counties and metropolitan counties in smaller metropolitan areas were excluded from the sample. More than 183 million Americans, nearly two-thirds of the U.S. population, lived in these 448 counties in 2000.

Six variables were part of the original county sprawl index (as shown in Table 1.1). U.S. Census data were used to derive three population density measures for each county:

- gross population density in persons per square mile, excluding rural census tracts with fewer than 100 persons per square mile (popden);
- percentage of the county population living at low suburban densities, specifically, densities between 100 and 1,500 persons per square mile, corresponding to less than one housing unit per acre (lt1500);
- percentage of the county population living at medium to high urban densities, specifically, more than 12,500 persons per square mile, corresponding to about eight housing units per acre, the lower limit of density needed to support mass transit (gt12500).

In deriving population density measures, census tracts were excluded if they had fewer than 100 residents per square mile (corresponding to rural areas, desert tracts, and other undeveloped lands). Ewing et al. were only concerned with sprawl in developed areas where the vast majority of residents live.

A fourth density variable was derived from estimated urban land area for each county from the National Resources Inventory of the U.S. Department of Agriculture: net population density of urban places within the county (urbden).

Data reflecting street accessibility for each county were also obtained from the U.S. Census. Street accessibility is related to block size since smaller blocks translate into shorter and more direct routes. A census block is defined as a statistical area bounded on all sides by streets, roads, streams, railroad tracks, or geopolitical boundary lines, in most cases. A traditional urban neighborhood is composed of intersecting bounding streets that form a grid, with houses built on the four sides of the block, facing these streets. The length of each side of that block, and therefore its block size, is relatively small. By contrast, a contemporary suburban neighborhood does not make connections between adjacent cul-de-sacs or loop roads. Instead, local streets only connect with the street at the subdivision entrance, which is on one side of the block boundary. Thus, the length of a side of this block is quite large, and the block itself often encloses multiple subdivisions to form a superblock, a half mile or more on a side. Large block sizes indicate a relative paucity of street connections and alternate routes.

Two street accessibility variables were computed for each county: average block size (avgblk) and percentage of blocks with areas less than 1/100 square mile, the size of a typical traditional urban block bounded by sides just over 500 feet in length (smlblk). Blocks larger than one square mile were excluded from these calculations, since they were likely to be in rural or other undeveloped areas.

The six variables were combined into one factor representing the degree of sprawl within the county. This was accomplished via principal component analysis, an analytical technique that takes a large number of correlated variables and extracts a small number of factors that embody the common variance in the original dataset. The extracted factors, or principal components, are weighted combinations of the original variables. When a variable is given a great deal of weight in constructing a principal component, we say that the variable loads heavily on that component. The greater the correlation between an original variable and a principal component, the greater the loading and the more weight the original variable is given in the overall principal component score. The more highly correlated the original variables, the more variance is captured by a single principal component.

The principal component selected to represent sprawl was the one capturing the largest share of common variance among the six variables, that is, the one upon which the observed variables loaded most heavily. This one component accounted for almost two-thirds of the variance in the dataset. Because this component captured the majority of the combined variance of these variables, no subsequent components were considered.

To arrive at a final index, Ewing et al. transformed the principal component, which had a mean of 0 and standard deviation of 1, to a scale with a mean of 100 and standard deviation of 25. This transformation produced a more familiar metric (like an IQ scale) and ensured that all values would be positive, thereby allowing us to take natural logarithms and estimate elasticities.

The bigger the value of the index, the more compact the county. The smaller the value, the more sprawling the county. Scores ranged from a high of 352 to a low of 63. At the most compact end of the scale were four New York City boroughs: Manhattan, Brooklyn, Bronx, and Queens; San Francisco County; Hudson County (Jersey City); Philadelphia County; and Suffolk County (Boston). At the most sprawling end of the scale were outlying counties of metropolitan areas in the Southeast and Midwest such as Goochland County in the Richmond, VA metropolitan area and Geauga County in the Cleveland, OH metropolitan area. The county sprawl index was positively skewed. Most counties clustered around intermediate levels of sprawl. In the U.S., few counties approach the densities of New York or San Francisco.

For these counties, the original sprawl index was validated against journey to work, adult obesity, and traffic fatality data (Ewing et al. 2003a; 2003b; 2003c). Later, the same county sprawl index was used to model the built environment in a study of youth obesity (Ewing et al. 2006). For that study, the index was computed for additional counties or county equivalents in order to have sprawl data for more National Longitudinal Survey of Youth (NLSY97) respondents. The 954 counties or county equivalents in the expanded sample represented the vast majority of counties lying within U.S. metropolitan areas, as defined by the U.S. Census Bureau in December 2003. Almost 82 percent of the U.S. population lived in metropolitan counties for which county sprawl indices were then available. Most recent research on sprawl and its impacts has made use of this expanded dataset.

Update to 2010

In updating the original county sprawl index to 2010, five of the six variables were derived in the exact same way as for 1990 and 2000. U.S. Census files for summary levels 140 (census tracts) and 101 (census blocks) were downloaded from American FactFinder. Population data were extracted for all census tracts in all metropolitan counties. Land area data were extracted for all census blocks in all metropolitan counties. Ninety-nine metropolitan counties were lost to the sample because they had no census tracts averaging 100 persons per square mile or more. They were deemed to be rural.

The sixth variable, net density of urban areas within the county, was originally computed using data on "urban and built up uses" from the National Resources Inventory (NRI) of the U.S. Department of Agriculture. The most recent NRI (2007) does not provide data at the county level. Therefore the U.S. Geological Survey's National Land Cover Database (NLCD) was used instead. NLCD serves as the definitive Landsat-based, 30-meter resolution, land cover database for the nation. It is a raster dataset providing spatial reference for land surface classification (for example, urban, agriculture, forest). It can be geo-processed to any geographic unit.

For the current work, the urban land area was generated at the county level using NLCD 2006 (the latest product) and county geography (2010) for the entire U.S. Using the "Tabulate Area" spatial analyst tool within ArcGIS, urban land areas within each county were calculated. The noncontiguous areas in the same county were aggregated resulting in total urban area in square miles. The value codes treated as urban were:

21. Developed, Open Space – Areas with a mixture of some constructed materials, but mostly vegetation in the form of lawn grasses. Impervious surfaces account for less than 20 percent of total cover. These areas most commonly include large-lot single-family housing units, parks, golf courses, and vegetation planted in developed settings for recreation, erosion control, or aesthetic purposes.

22. Developed, Low Intensity – Areas with a mixture of constructed materials and vegetation. Impervious surfaces account for 20 percent to 49 percent of total cover. These areas most commonly include single-family housing units.

23. Developed, Medium Intensity – Areas with a mixture of constructed materials and vegetation. Impervious surfaces account for 50 percent to 79 percent of the total cover. These areas most commonly include single-family housing units.

24. High Intensity – Highly developed areas where people reside or work in high numbers. Examples include apartment complexes, row houses, and commercial/industrial uses. Impervious surfaces account for 80 percent to 100 percent of the total cover.

Updated County Sprawl Index

The NRI and NLCD datasets are fairly comparable (see NIH website at http://gis.cancer.gov/tools/urban-sprawl/), making the county sprawl indices for 1990, 2000, and 2010 fairly comparable. However, NLCD is only available for the continental U.S. Therefore counties and county equivalents from Alaska, Hawaii, and Puerto Rico, 72 in total, were lost to the sample.

Once again, principal component analysis was used to reduce the six variables to a single index. This index accounts for 59 percent of the variance in the original six variables. Factor loadings are shown in Table 2.1.

We transformed the overall compactness score into an index with a mean of 100 and a standard deviation of 25. This was done for the sake of consistency and ease of understanding. With this transformation, the more compact counties have index values above 100, while the more sprawling have values below 100. County sprawl (compactness) indices were derived for 994 county and county equivalents in 2010. The 10 most compact and 10 most sprawling counties are shown in Tables 2.2 and 2.3. The most compact counties are as expected, central counties of large, older metropolitan areas. The most sprawling counties are outlying counties of large metropolitan areas, or component counties of smaller metropolitan areas. Values range from 54 for Jackson County outside Topeka, Kansas, the most sprawling county in 2010, to 464 for New York County (Manhattan), the most compact county in 2010. The NIH website also contains estimates of county sprawl in 2000, derived by applying the 2010 component score coefficient values to data for counties in 2000. It also presents changes in country sprawl, measured equivalently, between the two census years.

Table 2.1: County Sprawl Index Variables and Factor Loadings in 2010

Observed variable	Factor loading*
popden	0.858
lt1500	−0.658
gt12500	0.821
urbden	0.876
avgblk	−0.664
smlblk	0.711
Eigenvalue	3.56
Explained variance	59.3%

* Correlation with county sprawl index

Table 2.2: 10 Most Compact Counties in 2010 According to the Six Variable Index

	County	Metropolitan Area	Index
1	New York County, NY	New York-Northern New Jersey-Long Island, NY-NJ-PA	463.9
2	Kings County, NY	New York-Northern New Jersey-Long Island, NY-NJ-PA	341.4
3	Bronx County, NY	New York-Northern New Jersey-Long Island, NY-NJ-PA	331.5
4	Queens County, NY	New York-Northern New Jersey-Long Island, NY-NJ-PA	272.1
5	San Francisco County, CA	San Francisco-Oakland-Fremont, CA	247.8
6	Hudson County, NJ	New York-Northern New Jersey-Long Island, NY-NJ-PA	228.8
7	Suffolk County, MA	Boston-Cambridge-Quincy, MA-NH	217.1
8	Philadelphia County, PA	Philadelphia-Camden-Wilmington, PA-NJ-DE-MD	216.8
9	District of Columbia, DC	Washington-Arlington-Alexandria, DC-VA-MD-WV	193.3
10	Richmond County, NY	New York-Northern New Jersey-Long Island, NY-NJ-PA	190.1

Table 2.3: 10 Most Sprawling Counties in 2010 According to the Six Variable Index

		Metropolitan Area	Index
985	Ford County, IL	Champaign-Urbana, IL	67.3
986	Osage County, KS	Topeka, KS	66.9
987	Jasper County, IN	Chicago-Joliet-Naperville, IL-IN-WI	66.8
988	Grant County, AR	Little Rock-North Little Rock-Conway, AR	66.8
989	Tipton County, IN	Kokomo, IN	66.4
990	Chester County, TN	Jackson, TN	65.4
991	Morrow County, OH	Columbus, OH	63.4
992	Greene County, NC	Greenville, NC	63.3
993	Polk County, MN	Grand Forks, ND-MN	61.1
994	Jackson County, KS	Topeka, KS	54.6

Updated County Sprawl Index

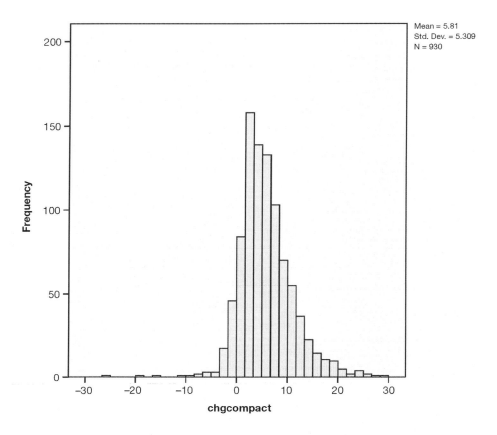

Figure 2.1: Scatterplot of 2010 Sprawl Index vs. 2000 Sprawl Index (Estimated Equivalently)

Figure 2.1 is a plot of 2010 sprawl index values vs. 2000 sprawl index values computed with the same component score coefficient values. As one would expect, the degree of county sprawl does not change dramatically over a 10-year period. Figure 2.2 is a histogram of changes in county sprawl values between 2000 and 2010, where 2000 sprawl values are computed using the 2010 component score coefficient values. As one would expect, given their fixed boundaries, most counties become more compact (denser and with smaller blocks) over the 10-year period. Sprawl occurs mainly as previously rural counties (in 2000) outside metropolitan areas become low-density suburbs and exurbs of metropolitan areas (in 2010).

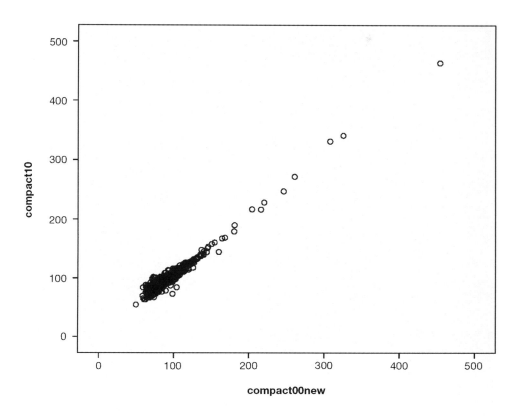

Figure 2.2: Histogram of Changes in County Sprawl Index Between 2000 and 2010 (Estimated Equivalently)

References

Ewing, R., Pendall, R., and Chen, D. (2003a). Measuring sprawl and its transportation impacts. *Transportation Research Record*, 1832, 175–183.

Ewing, R., Schmid, T., Killingsworth, R., Zlot, A., and Raudenbush, S. (2003b). Relationship between urban sprawl and physical activity, obesity, and morbidity. *American Journal of Health Promotion*, 18, 47–57.

Ewing, R., Schieber, R., and Zegeer. C. (2003c). Urban sprawl as a risk factor in motor vehicle occupant and pedestrian fatalities. *American Journal of Public Health*, 93, 1541–1545.

Ewing R., Brownson, R., and Berrigan, D. (2006). Relationship between urban sprawl and weight of U.S. youth. *American Journal of Preventive Medicine*, 31, 464–474.

Chapter Three

Refined County Sprawl Measures

A literature review by Ewing (1997) found poor accessibility to be the common denominator of sprawl. Sprawl is viewed as any development pattern in which related land uses have poor access to one another, leaving residents with no alternative to long-distance trips by automobile. Compact development, the polar opposite, is any development pattern in which related land uses are highly accessible to one another, thus minimizing automobile travel and attendant social, economic, and environmental costs. The following patterns are most often identified in the literature: scattered or leapfrog development, commercial strip development, uniform low-density development, or single-use development (with different land uses segregated from one another, as in bedroom communities). In scattered or leapfrog development, residents and service providers must pass by vacant land on their way from one developed use to another. In classic strip development, the consumer must pass other uses on the way from one store to the next; it is the antithesis of multipurpose travel to an activity center. Of course, in low-density, single-use development, everything is far apart due to large private land holdings and segregated land uses.

While the technical literature on sprawl focuses on land use patterns that produce poor regional accessibility, poor accessibility is also a product of fragmented street networks that separate urban activities more than need be. When asked, planners now routinely associate sprawl with sparse street networks as well as dispersed land-use patterns.

The original county sprawl index operationalized only two dimensions of urban form—residential density and street accessibility. Our grants from the NIH and Ford Foundation provide for the development of refined measures of county compactness or, conversely, county sprawl. These measures are modeled after the more complete metropolitan sprawl indices developed by Ewing et al.

(2002). The refined indices operationalize four dimensions, thereby characterizing county sprawl in all its complexity. The four are density, mix, centering, and street accessibility. The dimensions of the new county indices parallel the metropolitan indices, basically representing the relative accessibility provided by the county.

The full set of variables was used to derive a refined set of compactness/sprawl factors using principal component analysis. One principal component represents population density, another land use mix, a third centering, and a fourth street accessibility. County principal component values, standardized such that the mean value of each is 100 and the standard deviation is 25, are presented on the NIH website. The simple structure of the original county sprawl index has become more complex, but also more nuanced and comprehensive, in line with definitions of sprawl in the technical literature.

Density

Low residential density is on everyone's list of sprawl indicators. Our first four density variables are the same as in the original sprawl index, gross density of urban and suburban census tracts (popden), percentage of the population living at low suburban densities (lt1500), percentage of the population living at medium to high urban densities (gt12500), and urban density based on the National Land Cover Database (urbden).

The fifth density variable is analogous to the first, except it is derived with employment data from the Local Employment Dynamics (LED) database rather than population data from the 2010 Census. The LED database is assembled by the Census Bureau through a voluntary partnership with state labor market information agencies. The data provide unprecedented details about America's jobs, workers, and local economies. The LED data, available from 2002 to 2010, are collected at census block geography level and can be aggregated to any larger geography, in this case block groups. LED variables include total number of jobs, average age of workers, monthly earnings, and as of 2009 sex, race, ethnicity, and education levels. In this case, LED data were processed for the year 2010. The data were aggregated from census block geography to census block group geography to generate total jobs by two-digit NAICS code for every block group in the nation, except those in Massachusetts, which doesn't participate in the program. The density variable derived from the LED database is: gross employment density of urban and suburban census tracts (empden).

Principal components were extracted from the five density-related variables, and the principal component that accounted for the greatest variance became

Refined County Sprawl Measures

the county density factor. Factor loadings (that is, correlations of these variables with the density factor) are shown in Table 3.1. The eigenvalue of the density factor is 3.56, which means that this one factor accounts for more of the variance in the original dataset than three of the component variables combined. In other words, the density factor accounts for more than 70 percent of the total variance in the dataset. As expected, one of the variables loads negatively on the density factor, that being the percentage of population living at less than 1,500 persons per square mile. The rest load positively. Thus, for all component variables, higher densities translate into higher values of the density factor.

Mixed-Use

Three types of mixed-use measures are found in the land use-travel literature: those representing relative balance between jobs and population within subareas of a region; those representing the diversity of land uses within subareas of a region; and those representing the accessibility of residential uses to non-residential uses at different locations within a region. In this study, all three types were estimated for counties in our sample and became part of a mix factor.

The first two variables were calculated for each block group using block-level population data from the 2010 Census, and block-level employment data from the 2010 LED database. For the first variable, each block group centroid was buffered with a one-mile ring, and jobs and population were summed for blocks within the ring. One-mile rings were used to standardize geography for census block groups, which vary widely in size, making balance easier to achieve in the larger block groups. The resulting job and population totals were used to

Table 3.1: Variable Loadings on the County Density Factor for 2010

Observed variable	Factor loading*
popden	0.983
lt1500	0.848
gt12500	−0.440
urbden	0.850
empden	0.977
Eigenvalue	3.56
Explained variance	71.1%

* Correlation with the density factor

compute a job–population balance measure.[1] This variable equals 1 for block groups with the same ratio of jobs-to-residents within the one-mile ring as the metropolitan area as a whole; 0 for block groups with only jobs or residents within the one-mile ring, not both; and intermediate values for intermediate cases. All values were weighted by the sum of block group jobs and residents as a percentage of the county total to obtain countywide average job–population balance (jobpop).

For the second mixed-use variable, each block group centroid was again buffered with a one-mile ring, and jobs by sector were summed for blocks within the ring. An entropy formula was then used to compute a measure of job mix.[2] The variable equals 1 for block groups with equal numbers of jobs in each sector within the ring; 0 for block groups with all jobs in a single sector within the ring; and intermediate values for intermediate cases. The sectors considered in this case were retail, entertainment, health, education, and personal services. Values were weighted by the sum of block group population and employment as a percentage of the county total to obtain: countywide degree of job mixing (jobmix).

A third mixed-use variable uses data from Walk Score, Inc. to measure proximity to amenities, with different amenities weighted differently and amenities discounted as the distance to them increases up to one and a half miles, where they are assumed to be no longer accessible on foot.[3] Classic Walk Score data were acquired for all urban census tracts in the U.S. Year 2012 data were purchased to reduce the cost of data acquisition. Values were weighted by the sum of block group population and employment as a percentage of the county total to obtain: countywide average Walk Score (walkscore).

Principal components were extracted from the three mix-related variables, and the principal component that accounted for the greatest variance became

Table 3.2: Variable Loadings on the County Mix Factor for 2010

Observed variable	Factor loading*
jobpop	0.891
jobmix	0.942
walkscore	0.784
Eigenvalue	2.30
Explained variance	76.6%

* Correlation with the mix use factor

Refined County Sprawl Measures

the mix factor. Loadings of these variables on the mix factor are shown in Table 3.2. The eigenvalue of the mix factor is 2.30, which means that this one factor accounts for more than three-quarters of the total variance.

Centering

Urban centers are concentrations of activity that provide agglomeration economies, support alternative modes and multipurpose trip making, create a sense of place in the urban landscape, and otherwise differentiate compact urban areas from sprawling ones. Centeredness can exist with respect to population or employment, and with respect to a single dominant center or multiple subcenters. The technical literature associates compactness with centers of all types, and sprawl with the absence of centers of any type.

Ewing et al. (2002) measured metropolitan centering, in part, in terms of concentrations of development in or around historic CBDs of metropolitan areas. This concept of centering does not make much sense when applied to the individual counties that make up a metropolitan area, only one of which can contain the historic central business district. Other counties have their own subcenters in the polycentric metropolitan areas of today, and the existence of and proximity to these are what distinguish counties with concentrations of activity from those without. Four measures of centering were derived for metropolitan counties.

The first centering measure came straight out of the 2010 Census: coefficient of variation in census block group population densities, defined as the standard deviation of block group densities divided by the average density of block groups. The more variation in densities around the mean, the more centering and/or subcentering exists within the county (varpop).

The second centering measure was derived from the LED database and is analogous to the first measure, except for its use of employment density by block group rather than population density to compute: coefficient of variation in census block group employment densities, defined as the standard deviation of block group densities divided by the average density of block groups. The more variation in densities around the mean, the more centering and/or subcentering exists within the county (varemp).

The last two centering variables measure the proportion of employment and population within CBDs and employment subcenters. We first identified the location of CBDs and employment subcenters for all metropolitan areas. For identifying CBDs, we ran a local spatial autocorrelation procedure using the local Moran's I statistic (Anselin 1995).[4] With this procedure, it is possible to quantify the degree of clustering of neighboring zones with high levels of density. This method has been used by Baumont and Le Gallo (2003) and Riguelle et al. (2007).

Having CBDs for 356 metropolitan areas, we identified employment subcenters as the positive residuals estimated from an exponential employment density function using geographically weighted regression (GWR) method.[5] Using this procedure, we found 224 metropolitan areas to be monocentric (have only one center), 132 to be polycentric (have more than one center), and 18 metropolitan areas to be dispersed (have no CBD and no subcenter). This procedure resulted in two new centering variables. These findings were validated by inspecting Google Earth satellite images to identify concentrations of activity, and see whether they corresponded to our findings with GWR: percentage of county population in CBD or subcenters (popcen) and percentage of county employment in CBD or subcenters (empcen).

Principal components were extracted from the set of centering variables, and the principal component that accounted for the greatest variance became our centering factor. All component variables loaded positively on the centering factor (see Table 3.3). The eigenvalue of the centering factor is 1.96, which means that this one factor accounts for just under half of the total variance in the dataset.

Street Connectivity

In the refined sprawl indices, two street variables are the same as in the original county sprawl index: average block size excluding rural blocks of more than one square mile (avgblk) and percentage of small urban blocks of less than one hundredth of a square mile (smlblk). To these, two street connectivity variables were added. The two new street variables are: intersection density for urban and

Table 3.3: Variable Loadings on the County Centering Factor for 2010

Observed variable	Factor loading*
varpop	0.085
varemp	0.642
popcen	0.820
empcen	0.932
Eigenvalue	1.96
Explained variance	49.1%

* Correlation with the centering factor

Refined County Sprawl Measures

suburban census tracts within the county, excluding rural tracts with gross densities of less than 100 persons per square mile (intden) and percentage of four-or-more-way intersections, again excluding rural tracts (4-way).

Intersection density captures both block length and street connectivity. Percentage of four-or-more-way intersections provides a pure measure of street connectivity, as four-way intersections provide more routing options than three-way intersections.

Starting with a 2006 national dataset of street centerlines generated by TomTom that ships with ArcGIS, we produced a national database of street intersection locations, including for each intersection feature a count of streets that meet there. The TomTom dataset includes one centerline feature for each road segment running between neighboring intersections; i.e. every intersection is the spatially coincident endpoint of three or more road segments.[6]

The resulting national intersection database contains 13.1 million features; 77 percent of these are three-way intersections, and the remaining 23 percent are four-or-more-way intersections. Total counts of three- and four-or-more-way intersections were tabulated for census tracts, and census tracts were aggregated to obtain county-level data. For each county, the total number of intersections in urban and suburban tracts was divided by the land area to obtain intersection density (intden), while the number of four-or-more-way intersections was multiplied by 100 and divided by the total number of intersections to obtain the percentage of four-or-more way intersections (4-way).

Principal components were extracted from the full set of street-related variables, and the principal component that accounted for the greatest variance became our street connectivity factor. Loadings of these variables on the street factor are shown in Table 3.4. The eigenvalue of the street factor is 2.39, which

Table 3.4: Variable Loadings on the County Street Factor for 2010

Observed variable	Factor loading*
avgblk	−0.764
smlblk	0.901
inden	0.836
4-way	0.545
Eigenvalue	2.39
Explained variance	59.8%

* Correlation with the street factor

means that this one factor accounts for more than half of the total variance in the dataset. As expected, one of the variables loads negatively on the street connectivity factor, that being the average block size. The rest load positively. Thus, for all component variables, more connectivity translates into higher values of the street factor.

Relationship Among Compactness Factors

It has been said that measures of the built environment are so highly correlated that they should not be represented separately, but instead should be combined into a single index. Thus, for example, overall measures of walkability have been advanced as an alternative to individual measures.

This position is not borne out by this study, at least not at the county level. While correlated, as one might expect, the four compactness factors seem to represent distinct constructs. Their simple correlation coefficients are shown in Table 3.5. The highest is 0.647, which means that each factor explains less than 42 percent of the variation in the other.

Composite Index

The next issue we had to wrestle with was how to combine the four factors into a single sprawl index. A priori, there is no "right" way to do so, only ways that have more or less face validity.

Should the four factors be weighted equally, or should one or another be given more weight than the others? Density has certainly received more attention as an aspect of sprawl than has, say, street connectivity. However, beyond play in the literature, we could think of no rationale for differential weights. The first three factors all contribute to the accessibility or inaccessibility of different development patterns, none presumptively more than the others.

Table 3.5: Simple Pearson Correlation Between Four Factors

	Density factor	Mix factor	Centering factor	Street factor
Density factor	1	0.399**	0.523**	0.583**
Mix factor	0.399**	1	0.421**	0.647**
Centering factor	0.523**	0.421**	1	0.438**
Street factor	0.583**	0.647**	0.438**	1

** Significant at the 0.001 level

Refined County Sprawl Measures

Depending on their values, all move a county along the continuum from sprawl to compact development. Thus they were simply summed, in effect giving each dimension of sprawl equal weight in the overall index.

As with the individual sprawl factors, we transformed the overall compactness score into an index with a mean of 100 and a standard deviation of 25. This was done for the sake of consistency and ease of understanding. With this transform–ation, the more compact counties have index values above 100, while the more sprawling have values below 100.

Note that Massachusetts counties are missing from the mix factor and overall index for lack of LED data. The 10 most compact and 10 most sprawling counties are shown in Tables 3.6 and 3.7. The rankings are similar to those with the original county sprawl index. The most compact counties are central counties of large, older metropolitan areas. The most sprawling counties are outlying counties of large metropolitan areas, or component counties of smaller metropolitan areas. Values range from 45.5 for Oglethorpe County outside Athens, GA, the most sprawling county in 2010, to 425.2 for New York County, the borough of Manhattan.

Table 3.6: 10 Most Compact Counties in 2010 According to the Four-Factor Index (excluding Massachusetts counties)

	County	Metropolitan area	Index
1	New York County, NY	New York-Northern New Jersey-Long Island, NY-NJ-PA	425.2
2	Kings County, NY	New York-Northern New Jersey-Long Island, NY-NJ-PA	265.2
3	San Francisco County, CA	San Francisco-Oakland-Fremont, CA	251.3
4	Bronx County, NY	New York-Northern New Jersey-Long Island, NY-NJ-PA	224.0
5	Philadelphia County, PA	Philadelphia-Camden-Wilmington, PA-NJ-DE-MD	207.2
6	District of Columbia, DC	Washington-Arlington-Alexandria, DC-VA-MD-WV	206.4
7	Queens County, NY	New York-Northern New Jersey-Long Island, NY-NJ-PA	204.2
8	Baltimore city, MD	Baltimore-Towson, MD	190.9
9	Norfolk city, VA	Virginia Beach-Norfolk-Newport News, VA-NC	179.6
10	Hudson County, NJ	New York-Northern New Jersey-Long Island, NY-NJ-PA	178.7

Refined County Sprawl Measures

Table 3.7: 10 Most Sprawling Counties in 2010 According to the Four-Factor Index (excluding Massachusetts counties)

	County	Metropolitan area	Index
960	Spencer County, KY	Louisville/Jefferson County, KY-IN	60.4
961	Morrow County, OH	Columbus, OH	58.8
962	Brown County, IN	Indianapolis-Carmel, IN	58.5
963	Blount County, AL	Birmingham-Hoover, AL	56.6
964	Greene County, NC	Greenville, NC	56.6
965	Harris County, GA	Columbus, GA-AL	55.1
967	Macon County, TN	Nashville-Davidson—Murfreesboro—Franklin, TN	54.3
966	Elbert County, CO	Denver-Aurora-Broomfield, CO	54.3
968	Grant Parish, LA	Alexandria, LA	53.8
969	Oglethorpe County, GA	Athens-Clarke County, GA	45.5

Looking at Tables 2.2 and 3.6, it would seem that the original and new compactness indices are measuring the same construct, but that is not quite true. Just compare Tables 2.3 and 3.7, where there is no overlap in the most sprawling counties according to the two indices. The original compactness index is dominated by density variables (four of six variables in the index) and only slightly diluted by street variables (two of the six), which correlate strongly with density. The new compactness index dilutes the role of density by adding two new factors (mix and centering). The simple correlation coefficient between original and new indices is 0.865, which means that about 25 percent of the variance in each index is unexplained by the other. We would expect that they have similar but not identical relationships to outcome variables, and similar but not identical predictive power.

Greater Validity of New Index

Compared to the original county compactness index, the new four-factor index has greater construct and face validity. It has greater construct validity because it captures four different dimensions of the construct "compactness" (density, mix, centering, and street connectivity), whereas the original index captures only two dimensions (density and street connectivity).

Refined County Sprawl Measures

Figure 3.1: Most Compact County According to Both Indices (New York County, NY)

The greater face validity of the new four-factor index requires some explanation. The very first county compactness indices were derived for only 448 counties in the largest 101 metropolitan areas. The most sprawling counties, such as Geauga County outside Cleveland, have classic sprawl patterns of low-density suburban development.

Expanding to 994 counties and adding smaller metropolitan areas, the picture becomes more complicated. Tables 2.2 and 3.6 list the most compact counties as measured by both indices. The 10 most compact counties based on the original index largely overlap with the top 10 based on the new index (with the notable exception of Suffolk County (Boston), for which we don't have all required variables). New York County (Manhattan) is the most compact according to both indices (see Figure 3.1). Kings County (Brooklyn) is the second most compact according to both indices (see Figure 3.2).

Refined County Sprawl Measures

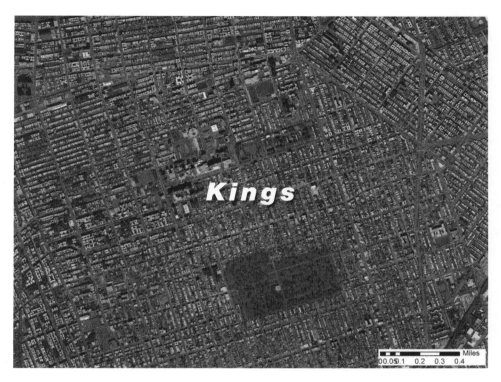

Figure 3.2: Second Most Compact County According to Both Indices (Kings County, NY)

However, the 10 most sprawling counties are entirely different when measured by different indices (see Tables 2.3 and 3.7). Which index has greater face validity? We reviewed satellite imagery for the 10 most sprawling counties, according to both indices, and found that the development patterns for the new index are much more representative of classic suburban sprawl (see Tables 3.8 and 3.9). While all 20 counties are part of metropolitan areas, many of the counties rated as most sprawling according to the original index have different development patterns than expected. They would best be described as exurban counties with small towns surrounded by farmlands (see Figures 3.3 and 3.4). The small towns have moderate densities and gridded streets. The fact they are part of larger census tracts, our units of analysis, depresses their densities and compactness scores. They are not examples of classic suburban or exurban sprawl. However, the counties rated as most sprawling according to the new four-factor index have census tracts with very low-density residential development.

33

Table 3.8: 10 Most Sprawling Counties in 2010 According to the Six-Variable Index

County	Development pattern	Index
Ford County, IL	**Small town surrounded by rural development**	67.3
Osage County, KS	**Small town surrounded by rural development**	66.9
Jasper County, IN	Continuous low density suburban development	66.8
Grant County, AR	Continuous low density suburban development	66.8
Tipton County, IN	**Small town surrounded by rural development**	66.4
Chester County, TN	Continuous low density suburban development	65.4
Morrow County, OH	Continuous low density suburban development	63.4
Greene County, NC	Continuous low density suburban development	63.3
Polk County, MN	**Small town surrounded by rural development**	61.1
Jackson County, KS	**Small town surrounded by rural development**	54.6

Figure 3.3: Most Sprawling County According to Six-Variable Index (Jackson County, KS)

Table 3.9: 10 Most Sprawling Counties in 2010 According to the Four-Factor Index (excluding Massachusetts counties)

County	Metropolitan area	Index
Spencer County, KY	Louisville/Jefferson County, KY-IN	60.4
Morrow County, OH	Columbus, OH	58.8
Brown County, IN	Indianapolis-Carmel, IN	58.5
Blount County, AL	Birmingham-Hoover, AL	56.6
Greene County, NC	Greenville, NC	56.6
Harris County, GA	Columbus, GA-AL	55.1
Macon County, TN	Nashville-Davidson—Murfreesboro—Franklin, TN	54.3
Elbert County, CO	Denver-Aurora-Broomfield, CO	54.3
Grant Parish, LA	Alexandria, LA	53.8
Oglethorpe County, GA	Athens-Clarke County, GA	45.5

Figure 3.4: Second Most Sprawling County According to Six-Variable Index (Polk County, MN)

Refined County Sprawl Measures

Figure 3.5: Most Sprawling County According to Four-Factor Index (Oglethorpe County, GA)

Figure 3.6: Second Most Sprawling County According to Four-Factor Index (Grant Parish, LA)

Notes

1 The equation used to calculate job–population balance was:

$$\sum_{i=0}^{i=n} (1-(ABS(J_i-JP^*P_i))/(J_i+JP^*P_i))^\star((BJ_i+BP_i)/(TJ+TP))$$

where:

i = census tract number (excluding those with fewer than 100 persons per square mile)

n = number of census tracts in the county

J = jobs in the census tract

P = residents in the census tract

JP = jobs per person in the metropolitan area

TJ = total jobs in the county

TP = total residents in the county

2 The equation for this measure is:

$$\sum_{i=1}^{n}\sum_{j} ((P_j^\star LN(P_j))/LN(j))^\star((BJ_i+BP_i)/(TJ+TP))$$

where:

i = census tract number (excluding those with fewer than 100 persons per square mile)

n = number of census tracts in the county

j = number of sectors

P_j = proportion of jobs in sector j

JP = jobs per person in the metropolitan area

TJ = total jobs in the county

TP = total residents in the county

3 A grocery store, for example, gets three times the weight of a book store. The distance decay function starts with a value of 100 and decays to 75 percent at a half mile, 12.5 percent at one mile, and zero at 1.5 miles.

Refined County Sprawl Measures

4   Local Moran's I is defined as:

$$I_i = \frac{(x_i - \bar{x})}{\sum_{i=1}^{n}(x_i - \bar{x})^2/n} \sum_{j=1}^{n} w_{ij}(x_j - \bar{x})$$

where I_i is the local Moran's I coefficient, X is the value of employment density, w_{ij} is the matrix of spatial weights, and n is the number of observations. Through calculating z-values of the local Moran statistic (see Anselin 1995; Getis and Ord 1996) it is then possible to identify two types of spatial clusters and two types of outliers:

- High–high   High values around neighbors with high values (cluster)
- Low–low   Low values around neighbors with low values (cluster)
- High–low   High values around neighbors with low values (outlier)
- Low–high   Low values around neighbors with high values (outlier)

Using LED data of block groups, the Moran's I analysis was done for all metropolitan areas. The high–high clusters with the highest employment density in each metropolitan statistical area (MSA) were considered as CBD candidates. However not all of them are CBDs. We excluded the hot spots containing large firms such as hospitals, malls, and university campuses by applying the threshold of having employment share of no more than 75 percent in each sector. We identified CBD for a total of 356 metropolitan areas.

5   GWR estimates a smoothed employment density surface using only nearby observations for any data point (block groups), with more weight given to closer observations. The dependent variable of the GWR estimations is employment density by block group and the independent variable is the distance of the block group centroid from the CBD. We used the Adaptive kernel type with 30 numbers of neighbors. The block groups with highest positive residual (if residual is four times greater than predicted) are candidates for employment subcenters. As with CBD identification, we excluded the block groups containing large firms such as hospitals, regional malls, and university campuses by applying the requirement that the employment share be no more than 75 percent in each sector. Finally we excluded cases when their ratio of employment to population was less than 2.5 (Gordon et al. 1986). We identified a total of 451 subcenters in 132 metropolitan areas.

6   Intersection features were created as follows: using Census Feature Class Code (CFCC) values, we filtered out all freeways, unpaved tracks, and other roadways that don't function as pedestrian routes. Divided roadways, which from a pedestrian mobility perspective function similarly to undivided roadways of the same functional class, were represented in the source data as pairs of (roughly) parallel centerline segments. These were identified by CFCC value and merged into single segments using GIS tools. Streets intersecting the original divided roadways were trimmed or extended to the new merged centerlines, and the new merged centerlines were split at each intersection with side streets such that centerline features only intersect each other at feature endpoints. Roundabouts were assumed to function similarly to single 4-or-more-way intersections, rather than close-set clusters of intersections joining the roundabout proper and the incoming streets. As such, centroids of roundabout circles were located and assigned an assumed count of four incoming streets; endpoints of incoming street features were ignored.

With the corrected street centerline data prepared, we generated point features at both endpoints of each street segment. Points closer together than 12 meters were adjusted to be spatially coincident in order to control for any possible remaining geometric errors related to divided roadways. We then used GIS tools to count the number of points (representing ends of street segments) coinciding at any location. Locations with point counts of one (dead ends) or two (locations where a roadway changes name, functional class, or other attribute) were discarded as non-street intersections. Remaining locations were flagged with attributes indicating whether a point was a three-way or a four-or-more-way intersection.

References

Anselin, L. (1995). Local indicators of spatial association—LISA. *Geographical Analysis*, 27(2), 93–115.

Baumont, C., and Le Gallo, J. (2003). 4 spatial convergence clubs and the European regional growth process, 1980. In Fingleton, B. (Ed.) *European Regional Growth* (pp. 131–158). Springer, Berlin Heidelberg.

Ewing, R. (1997). Is Los Angeles-style sprawl desirable? *Journal of the American Planning Association*, 63(1), 107–126.

Ewing, R., Pendall, R., and Chen, D. (2002). *Measuring Sprawl and Its Impacts*. Smart Growth America, Washington, D.C.

Getis, A., and Ord, J.K. (1996). Local spatial statistics: An overview. In Longley, P.A., and Batty, M. (Ed.) *Spatial Analysis: Modelling in a GIS Environment* (pp. 261–279). Wiley, Inc., New York.

Gordon, P., and Richardson, H.W. (1997). Are compact cities a desirable planning goal? *Journal of the American Planning Association*, 63(1), 95–106.

Gordon, P., Richardson, H.W., and Wong, H.L. (1986). The distribution of population and employment in a polycentric city: the case of Los Angeles. *Environment and Planning A*, 18(2), 161–173.

Riguelle, F., Thomas, I., and Verhetsel, A. (2007). Measuring urban polycentrism: A European case study and its implications. *Journal of Economic Geography*, 7(2), 193–215.

Chapter Four

Validation of County Sprawl Indices

The potential to moderate travel demand by changing the built environment is the most heavily researched subject in urban planning. The effect of the built environment on transportation and travel behavior is confirmed by more than 200 empirical studies (Ewing and Cervero 2010). This literature is summarized in recent reviews by Cao et al. (2009), Heath et al. (2006), Pont et al. (2009), Graham-Rowe et al. (2011), Litman and Steele (2011), and Salon et al. (2012), and in meta-analyses by Leck (2006) and Ewing and Cervero (2010).

In travel research, influences of the built environment on travel have often been named with words beginning with D. The original "three Ds," coined by Cervero and Kockelman (1997), are density, diversity, and design, followed later by destination accessibility and distance to transit (Ewing and Cervero 2001; 2010). While usually measured at the neighborhood scale, the D variables roughly correspond to our conception of sprawl at the larger scale of counties. Sprawl is any development pattern that is low on D variables (or high on distance to transit). Compact development is any development pattern with high D values (or inversely, low on distance to transit). Development density, a component of county compactness, precisely corresponds to density of neighborhoods, and is measured the same way. Land-use mix, a component of county compactness, precisely corresponds to land-use diversity of neighborhoods, and is measured the same way. Street connectivity, a component of county compactness, precisely corresponds to street network design, the most common design variable measured in travel behavior studies. Even centering, a component of county compactness, has a rough equivalency in the concept of destination accessibility. Thus to the extent that the travel behavior literature has established D variables as predictors of travel choices, we would expect to find a strong relationship between dimensions of sprawl and travel outcomes at the more aggregate scale of counties.

Validation of County Sprawl Indices

The relationships between sprawl and travel outcomes can be used to validate our county sprawl measures, and also to see if one measure has more predictive power than another. If sprawl has any consistently recognized outcome, it is automobile dependence. We would expect to find that, after controlling for other relevant influences, compact counties have relatively low vehicle ownership, high transit and walking commute mode shares, and short drive times to work.

Methods

Data and Variables

Using American Factfinder, we downloaded data from the 2010 American Community Survey (ACS), five-year estimates, and computed average vehicle ownership, mode shares, and average drive time by county. We also downloaded socioeconomic data and computed percentages and mean values to describe county populations. The ACS is an ongoing statistical survey that produces estimates of demographic, social, economic, and housing characteristics at a variety of geographic scales. The five-year estimates are based on data collected over a 60-month period from 2006 through 2010. From the 2010 Census, we downloaded data on gender, age, race, household type, and housing tenure, and computed percentages and mean values to describe county populations.

We also downloaded data on crime, weather/climate, fuel price, and the size of metropolitan area in which a county is located, all for 2010. Crime statistics came from the uniform crime report of the Federal Bureau of Investigation (FBI). The FBI supplied crimes by type (violent and property) and subtype (murder, rape, etc.) aggregated by county. Annual heating degree days (HDD), cooling degree days (CDD), and annual precipitation data came from the National Oceanic and Atmospheric Administration (NOAA)'s National Climatic Data Center for 2009 for HDD and 2010 for the other two variables. We recorded data for stations located in the same MSAs as the counties. In a few cases there were not weather stations in MSAs, so we used data from the closest station to a particular MSA. Gasoline price data at the MSA level were purchased from the Oil Price Information Service (OPIS). Retail prices are average prices from samples of gas stations in each MSA and are reported with all relevant taxes included. These prices are the true posted "sign" prices (as they would appear outside a gas station).

Table 4.1 provides a list of all dependent and independent variables. We estimated different models using different measures of compactness. Our first set of regressions used the same six-variable measure of compactness/sprawl as

Table 4.1: Variables Used to Explain Travel Outcomes (all variables log transformed)

Variables		Data sources
Level 1 Dependent variables (county level)		
hhveh	average household vehicle ownership	ACS 2006–2010
pctwalk	percentage of commuters walking to work	ACS 2006–2010
pcttrans	percentage of commuters using public transportation (excluding taxi)	ACS 2006–2010
drivetim	average journey-to-work drive time in minutes	ACS 2006–2010
Level 1 Independent variables (county level)		
pctmale	percentage of male population	Census 2010
pctwhite	percentage of white population	Census 2010
pct1524	percentage of population 15-24 years old	Census 2010
hhsize	average household size	Census 2010
hhinc	median household income	ACS 2006–2010
crime	violent crime rate per 100,000 population	FBI Uniform Crime Statistics
indexo	county compactness index for 2010 (using the same 2000 index variables)	computed
denfac	density factor (a weighted combination of five density variables)	Census 2010, NLCD database
mixfac	mix factor (a weighted combination of three mixed-use variables)	Census 2010, LED 2010, Walk Score
cenfac	centering factor (a weighted combination of four centering variables)	Census 2010, LED 2010
strfac	street factor (a weighted combination of four street-related variables)	Census 2010, TomTom, ESRI
indexn	county compactness index for 2010 (including additional variables compared to 2000 index)	computed
Level 2 Independent variables (metropolitan level)		
metpop	metropolitan area population	Census 2010
precip	annual precipitation (inches)	NOAA database 2010
hdd	heating degree-days: the outside base temperature above which a building needs heating	NOAA database 2010
cdd	cooling degree-days: the outside base temperature above which a building needs cooling	NOAA database 2010
fuel	average fuel price for the metropolitan area	OPIC database 2010

Validation of County Sprawl Indices

in 2000, but updated to 2010 (indexo). The second set of regressions used the new measure of compactness/sprawl, with four distinct factors combined into an overall compactness score (indexn). The third set of regressions used the four distinct factors individually as regressors (denfac, mixfac, cenfac, strfac).

Our dependent variables were logged so as to be normally distributed and hence properly modeled with regression analysis. Figures 4.1 and 4.2 show, respectively, histograms of the walk share of commute trips for counties in our sample, and the natural logarithm of walk share. The latter clearly conforms more closely to a normal distribution than does the former. The distribution is even more skewed for the transit share of commute trips, and so it too was logged. The distribution of average drive times comes closer to normality, but conforms more closely to a normal distribution when logged than when linear.

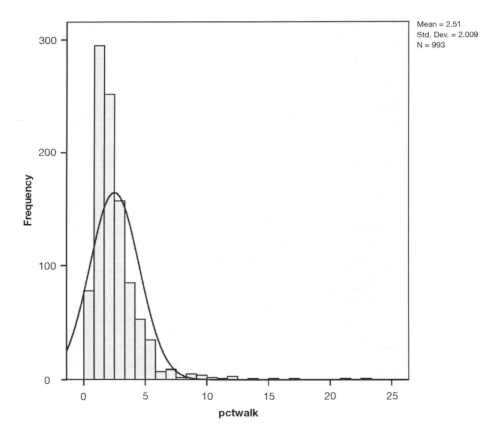

Figure 4.1: Frequency Distribution of the Percentage of Commute Walk Trips by County

Validation of County Sprawl Indices

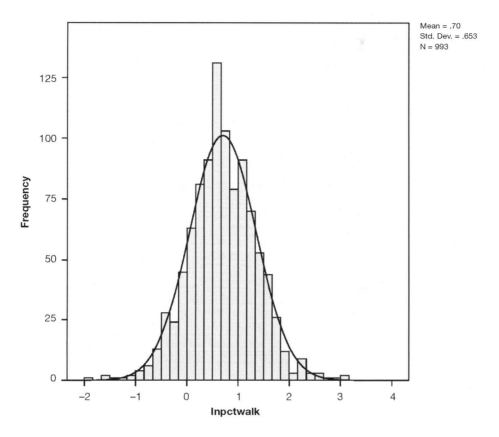

Figure 4.2: Frequency Distribution of the Natural Logarithm of the Percentage of Commute Walk Trips by County

As for the independent variables, we focus on the compactness/sprawl measures, as the other variables are simply used as controls. As shown in Figure 4.3, the natural logarithm of walk mode share, when plotted against the linear version of the original compactness index, suffers from nonlinearity, outlying values, and heteroskedasticity. All three statistical problems are moderated when, instead, the natural logarithm of the walk mode share is plotted against the natural logarithm of the compactness index, and the New York City cases are dropped from the sample, as in Figure 4.4. Therefore, in all regressions, we transformed all variables into log form to achieve a better fit with the data, reduce the influence of outliers, and adjust for nonlinearity of the data. The transformations had the added advantage of allowing us to interpret regression coefficients as elasticities. An elasticity is a percentage change in one variable

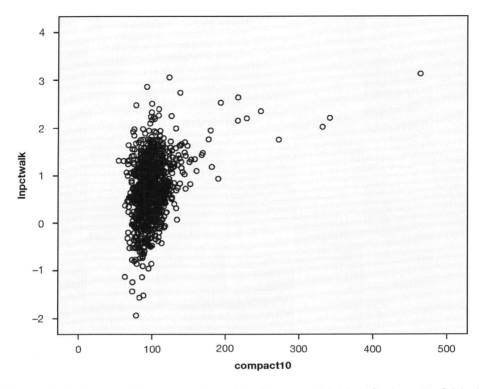

Figure 4.3: Scatterplot of Natural Logarithm of the Commute Walk Mode Share vs. the Original Compactness Index

that accompanies a 1 percent change in another variable. Elasticities are the most common measures of effect size in both economics and planning.

Analytical Method

As shown in Table 4.1, our independent variables come from two levels of geography, the county and the metropolitan area or MSA. Since all counties located in an MSA share characteristics of that MSA such as climate and fuel price, we can say that counties are "nested" within MSAs. This nesting tends to produce dependence among cases, violating the independence assumption of ordinary least squares regression or OLS. Standard errors of regression coefficients associated with MSA characteristics based on OLS will consequently be underestimated, and regression coefficients themselves will be inefficient.

Validation of County Sprawl Indices

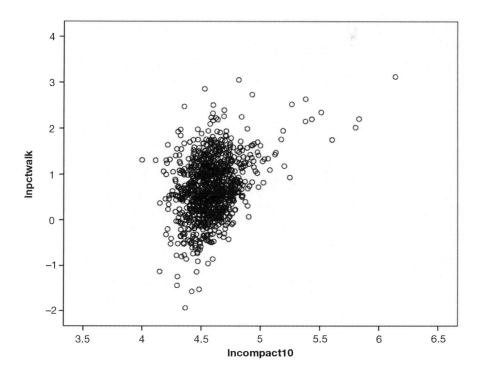

Figure 4.4: Scatterplot of Natural Logarithm of the Commute Walk Mode Share vs. the Natural Logarithm of Original Compactness Index

Whenever individuals or other entities are "nested" within higher-level units, hierarchical or multilevel modeling (MLM) methods are preferred for explaining individual outcomes in terms of both individual and group characteristics. Multilevel modeling overcomes the limitations of OLS, accounting for the dependence among lower level units and producing more accurate coefficient and standard error estimates. So MLM is used in this analysis for all transportation outcomes. Models were estimated with HLM 6.08.

Results

Household Vehicle Ownership

Results for household vehicle ownership are shown in Table 4.2. Average vehicle ownership is, as expected, directly related to household size, household income,

Validation of County Sprawl Indices

and percentage of whites in the population. Vehicle ownership is negatively related to average fuel price, doubtless because the generalized cost of automobile use is higher in metropolitan areas with higher fuel prices. Vehicle ownership is negatively related to CDDs. We would say this is because warm climates support walking and bicycling, but this explanation does not square with later results.

The variables of greatest interest—the original compactness index, the new compactness index, and the four individual compactness factors—are negatively related to household vehicle ownership (with the exception of the street factor, which is insignificant). A household of comparable socioeconomic status can make do with fewer cars in a compact county because vehicle trips are less numerous and shorter. This phenomenon is known as car shedding. Of the four compactness factors, the density factor has the strongest relationship to vehicle ownership. A dense urban environment usually offers alternatives to the automobile; the automobile has less utility in such an environment due to traffic congestion and parking problems. The centering factor is only slightly less significant than the density factor, and the mix factor less significant still.

Table 4.2: Relationships to Average Household Vehicle Ownership (log-log form with robust standard errors)

	Model 1			Model 2			Model 3		
	coeff.	t-ratio	p-value	coeff.	t-ratio	p-value	coeff.	t-ratio	p-value
constant	0.88	2.39	0.017	0.57	2.31	0.022	2.42	6.39	<0.001
hhsize	0.49	10.19	<0.001	0.43	8.17	<0.001	0.42	10.4	<0.001
hhinc	0.17	8.53	<0.001	0.15	7.40	<0.001	0.16	14.1	<0.001
pctwhite	0.099	4.74	<0.001	0.13	8.64	<0.001	0.069	4.46	<0.001
cdd	−0.034	−6.25	<0.001	−0.049	−6.51	<0.001	−0.04	−8.44	<0.001
fuel	−0.39	−4.41	<0.001	−0.47	−4.46	<0.001	−0.18	−2.46	0.014
indexo	−0.50	−5.29	<0.001						
indexn				−0.38	−5.41	<0.001			
denfac							−0.75	−7.69	<0.001
mixfac							−0.036	−2.60	0.010
cenfac							−0.058	−5.14	<0.001
strfac							0.017	0.70	0.49
pseudo-R2	NA*			NA*			NA*		

* The null model doesn't converge

Validation of County Sprawl Indices

Walk Mode Shares

Results for walking to work are shown in Table 4.3. Among the level 1 variables, walking to work is positively related to the percentage of young adults in the county population and the percentage of males. These relationships are as expected, as young people are less likely to have private vehicles available to them and more likely to be physically active. Males are less likely than females to be intimidated by environmental conditions such as crime. Walking to work is negatively related to household size and household income. These relationships are also as expected, since large households can make more efficient use of automobiles through trip chaining and carpooling and higher-income households own more private vehicles. Finally, walking to work is negatively related to the violent crime rate within the county. Crime has been found to discourage physical activity generally.

Among the level 2 variables, walking to work is positively related to metropolitan average fuel price and negatively related to cooling degree days. The first relationship reflects the depressing effect of higher fuel prices on auto use; there are persistent and significant differences in fuel prices across regions. The second relationship indicates that hot climates and weather discourage walking to work. This seems reasonable since the work trip tends to be longer than trips for other purposes, making environmental conditions especially important.

As for the variables of greatest interest to us, those related to the built environment, the original compactness index (indexo) in Model 1 has the expected strong positive relationship to walking. Compact counties, with high values of the index, have relatively high walk shares. As noted, the coefficients of these log–log models are elasticities. Every 1 percent increase in the original county compactness index results in a 0.54 percent increase in the walk mode share. The new compactness index (indexn) in Model 2 has an even stronger relationship to walking. The coefficient and t-statistic are higher for the new index than the original index. Every 1 percent increase in this index results in a 0.66 percent increase in the walk mode share.

The new multidimensional compactness factors are significant in two cases and have expected positive sign in three cases. The density factor, denfac, is the most important correlate of walking, followed by the mix factor, mixfac. A 1 percent increase in the density factor is associated with a 0.72 percent increase in walking, while a 1 percent increase in the mix factor is associated with a 0.25 percent increase in walking. The centering factor has a negative but insignificant relationship to walking. Population and employment centers may

Validation of County Sprawl Indices

have less balanced jobs and housing, making walk trips less practical. The big surprise is that the street factor is not significant. It is widely assumed that small blocks, frequent intersections, and high street connectivity translate into greater walkability. At least in this aggregate analysis, this does not appear to be the case.

Transit Mode Shares

Results for taking transit to work are shown in Table 4.4. Among the level 1 variables, transit use is positively related to the percentage of young adults in the county population. This relationship is as expected, as young people are less likely to have private vehicles available to them. Transit use is negatively related to the percentage of whites in the population, which may suggest a particular bias against transit for this racial group. Transit use is negatively related to average household size but positively related to household income, both at significant levels. The first relationship is as expected, since large households can make more efficient use of automobiles through trip chaining and carpooling. The second

Table 4.3: Relationships to Walk Mode Share (log-log form with robust standard errors)

	Model 1			Model 2			Model 3		
	coeff.	t-ratio	p-value	coeff.	t-ratio	p-value	coeff.	t-ratio	p-value
constant	−11.2	−3.87	<0.001	−14.6	−5.17	<0.001	−15.8	−4.76	<0.001
hhsize	−2.86	−10.0	<0.001	−2.56	−10.9	<0.001	−2.68	−10.0	<0.001
pctmale	2.29	3.33	0.001	3.29	5.01	<0.001	3.31	4.20	0.001
pct1524	1.29	18.4	<0.001	1.19	14.5	<0.001	1.21	15.7	<0.001
hhinc	−0.12	−1.30	0.20	−0.22	−2.44	0.015	−0.25	−2.75	0.007
crime	−0.051	−2.07	0.039	−0.082	−3.26	0.002	−0.079	−3.33	0.001
cdd	−0.18	−5.04	<0.001	−0.15	−4.42	<0.001	−0.16	−4.79	<0.001
fuel	2.70	5.27	<0.001	2.54	4.90	<0.001	2.40	4.83	<0.001
indexo	0.54	3.32	0.001						
indexn				0.66	6.59	<0.001			
denfac							0.72	2.58	0.010
mixfac							0.25	2.14	0.033
cenfac							−0.095	−1.08	0.28
strfac							0.16	1.28	0.20
pseudo-R2		0.37			0.37			0.38	

Validation of County Sprawl Indices

relationship is unexpected. Our initial assumption was that income and transit were positively related due to suburban commuters in large metropolitan areas such as New York and San Francisco commuting in large numbers by rail into the city. However, we found that the positive relationship extends to commuting by bus. So we must assume that the relationship is due to some confounding influence. Alternatively, it may be that after controlling for race, higher-income households actually consume more transit service.

Among the level 2 variables, transit use is positively related to metropolitan average fuel price, metropolitan population, and HDDs. The first relationship reflects the depressing effect of higher fuel prices on auto use; there are persistent and significant differences in fuel price across regions. The second relationship reflects both transportation supply and demand. Large metropolitan areas provide much more transit service than do small ones and are also more congested, which discourages auto use. The relationship to climate and weather is plausible. Cold climates and weather may encourage transit use as an alternative to walking greater distances.

As for the variables of greatest interest to us, the original compactness index (indexo) in Model 1 has the expected strong positive relationship to commuting by transit. Compact counties, with high values of the index, have much higher transit mode shares than do sprawling counties. The relationship is elastic. Every 1 percent increase in the county compactness index results in an almost 3 percent increase in the transit mode share. The new compactness index (indexn) also has a positive relationship to transit use, but a weaker one than that of the original index. The original index is dominated by density variables, and density is widely viewed as the *sine qua non* for high transit use. By contrast, the new index dilutes the effect of density by giving equal weight to mix, centering, and street accessibility.

The new multidimensional compactness factors have the expected signs and are significant in three cases. The density factor, denfac, has the highest elasticity and highest significance level. Every 1 percent increase in the density factor is associated with a 2.81 percent increase in transit mode share. The centering factor, cenfac, and street factor, strfac, are also significant with elasticities of 0.67 and 0.63, respectively. Activities are concentrated in centers, and hence easily served by transit. Grid-like street networks are more easily served by transit routes, and tend to shorten walking access distances. The mix factor is not significant, which flies in the face conventional wisdom but is consistent with some empirical research.

Validation of County Sprawl Indices

Table 4.4: Relationships to Transit Mode Share (log-log form with robust standard errors)

	Model 1			Model 2			Model 3		
	coeff.	t-ratio	p-value	coeff.	t-ratio	p-value	coeff.	t-ratio	p-value
constant	−34.1	−12.6	<0.001	−28.4	−10.5	<0.001	−38.9	−13.0	<0.001
hhsize	−2.42	−4.33	<0.001	−2.07	−3.59	0.001	−1.93	−3.32	0.001
hhinc	1.18	4.92	<0.001	1.02	4.14	<0.001	1.12	4.48	<0.001
pctwhite	−0.99	−5.66	<0.001	−1.09	−6.45	<0.001	−0.91	−5.13	<0.001
pct1524	1.24	7.47	<0.001	1.09	6.20	<0.001	1.11	6.43	<0.001
crime	0.11	2.35	0.019	0.053	1.09	0.28	0.074	1.57	0.12
metpop	0.12	3.97	<0.001	0.18	5.68	<0.001	0.13	3.83	<0.001
hdd	0.27	3.39	0.001	0.18	2.48	0.014	0.20	2.66	0.009
fuel	6.42	8.29	<0.001	5.71	7.19	<0.001	5.55	6.86	0.002
indexo	2.92	11.6	<0.001						
indexn				2.38	9.58	<0.001			
denfac							2.81	4.38	<0.001
mixfac							0.21	0.93	0.35
cenfac							0.67	4.41	<0.001
strfac							0.63	2.57	0.011
pseudo-R2		0.26			0.26			0.27	

Drive Times

Results for average drive times to work are shown in Table 4.5. Among the level 1 variables, average drive time to work is positively related to household size, negatively related to the percentage of young adults, and negatively related to household income. These relationships may be explained by household life styles and activity patterns. Larger households are more likely to trip chain and carpool on the way to work, and more likely to live in the suburbs where single-family housing is less expensive and schools are better. Young people living on their own can live close to work since they do not have to accommodate a working spouse or children. The negative relationship to household income is difficult to explain. We would have expected that higher-income households consume more residential space and hence live farther from work, consistent with economic theory. This result may be due to higher income households being able to afford housing closer to work, whereas lower-income households have to drive until they qualify for a mortgage. Or it may due to higher income

Validation of County Sprawl Indices

households actually living farther from work in distance, but traveling on suburban streets and highways at higher speeds with resulting shorter travel times to work.

Among the level 2 variables, larger metropolitan areas (measured in terms of population) generate longer commutes to work. This is consistent with the literature and common sense. The amount of annual precipitation is positively related to average drive time, which seems reasonable since vehicle speeds are lower under wet or icy conditions. The positive relationship to average fuel price is likely due to some confounding factor (perhaps a regional effect).

Also consistent with much of the literature is the negative relationship between average drive time and the original compactness index. Every 1 percent increase in the index is associated with a 0.40 percent decrease in drive time. The new compactness index is actually more significant than the original, and has a higher elasticity value. The new compactness index incorporates mixed use and centering variables, which should translate into better jobs–housing balance.

In the more fully specified model, three of four compactness factors have negative signs, though only two are statistically significant. The strongest influence is mixed use factor, followed by the centering factor. Activity centers, mixed uses, and fine street networks bring homes and work places closer together. The odd man out is density, which has a positive sign and is statistically significant. While higher density also brings homes closer to work places, it apparently creates enough congestion to partially offset that beneficial effect. This finding is consistent with some previous research.

Discussion

All measures of compactness have now been validated against journey-to-work data from the 2010 American Community Survey (2006–2010 average). As in 2003, we hypothesized that county compactness in 2010 would be directly related to the walk share of commute trips and the transit share of commute trips (after controlling for relevant covariates). County compactness was expected to be inversely related to average household vehicle ownership and average drive time to work. These relationships are confirmed. For all outcomes, sprawling counties perform less well than compact ones.

These results tend to validate our compactness/sprawl indices. They also suggest that the new compactness index has stronger and more significant relationships to walking and drive time than does the original compactness index. Only transit use favors the original index.

Validation of County Sprawl Indices

Table 4.5: Relationships to Average Drive Time (log–log form with robust standard errors)

	Model 1			Model 2			Model 3		
	coeff.	t–ratio	p-value	coeff.	t-ratio	p-value	coeff.	t-ratio	p-value
constant	3.81	11.85	<0.001	3.98	13.0	<0.001	2.82	7.74	<0.001
hhsize	0.51	6.58	<0.001	0.34	4.47	<0.001	0.38	4.93	<0.001
hhinc	−0.077	−2.526	0.012	−0.072	−2.38	0.018	0.005	0.018	0.86
pct1524	−0.21	−7.33	<0.001	−0.15	−5.77	<0.001	−0.12	−5.82	<0.001
metpop	0.083	14.6	<0.001	0.080	15.1	<0.001	0.068	12.9	<0.001
precip	0.061	3.59	0.001	0.042	2.57	0.011	0.040	2.64	0.009
fuel	0.24	1.98	0.048	0.44	3.58	0.001	0.55	4.75	<0.001
indexo	−0.29	−3.59	0.001						
indexn				−0.35	−7.09	<0.001			
denfac							0.128	2.20	0.028
mixfac							−0.36	−10.9	<0.001
cenfac							−0.036	−1.67	0.096
strfac							−0.029	−1.08	0.28
pseudo-R2	NA*			NA*			NA*		

* Pseudo-R2s are negative. A pseudo-R2 is not entirely analogous to R2 in linear regression, which can only assume positive values. One standard text on multilevel modeling notes that the variance can increase when variables are added to the null model. It goes on to say: "This is counter-intuitive, because we have learned to expect that adding a variable with decrease the error variance, or at least keep it at its current level… In general, we suggest not setting too much store by the calculation of [pseudo-R2s]" (Kreft and de Leeuw 1998, 119). For more discussion of negative pseudo-R2s, also see Snijders and Bosker (1999)

The four factors representing individual dimensions of sprawl have, in most cases, the expected relationships to transportation outcomes. They also have not only face and construct validity, but a measure of internal validity.

The main limitation of this analysis has to do with the data it employs. By necessity, the study uses highly aggregate data from a variety of sources that are not always consistent as to the area under study and time period. They are simply the best data available from national sources with sufficient breadth to provide a panoramic view of sprawl in the U.S. Results will have to be validated through follow–up work of a more focused nature.

References

Cao, X., Mokhtarian, P.L., and Handy, S.L. (2009). Examining the impacts of residential self–selection on travel behaviour: A focus on empirical findings. *Transport Reviews*, 29(3), 359–395.

Cervero, R., and Kockelman, K. (1997). Travel demand and the 3Ds: Density, diversity, and design. *Transportation Research Part D: Transport and Environment*, 2(3), 199–219.

Ewing, R., and Cervero, R. (2001). Travel and the built environment. *Transportation Research Record*, 1780, 87–114.

Ewing, R., and Cervero, R. (2010). Travel and the built environment: A meta-analysis. *Journal of the American Planning Association*, 76(3), 265–294.

Graham-Rowe, E., Skippon, S., Gardner, B., and Abraham, C. (2011). Can we reduce car use and, if so, how? A review of available evidence. *Transportation Research Part A: Policy and Practice*, 45(5), 401–418.

Heath, G.W., Brownson, R.C., Kruger, J., Miles, R., Powell, K.E., Ramsey, L.T., and the Task Force on Community Preventive Services (2006). The effectiveness of urban design and land use and transport policies and practices to increase physical activity: A systematic review. *Journal of Physical Activity and Health*, 3(1), 55–76.

Kreft, I., and de Leeuw, J. (1998). *Introducing Multilevel Modeling*. Sage Publications, Thousand Oaks, CA.

Leck, E. (2006). The impact of urban form on travel behavior: A meta-analysis. *Berkeley Planning Journal*, 19(1), 37–58.

Litman, T., and Steele, R. (2011). *Land Use Impacts On Transport: How Land Use Factors Affect Travel Behavior*, Victoria Transport Policy Institute (www.vtpi.org). Available online at: www.vtpi.org/landtravel.pdf (last accessed 5 May 2017).

Pont, K., Ziviani, J., Wadley, D., Bennett, S., and Abbott, R. (2009). Environmental correlates of children's active transportation: A systematic literature review. *Health & Place*, 15(3), 827–840.

Salon, D., Boarnet, M.G., Handy, S., Spears, S., and Tal, G. (2012). How do local actions affect VMT? A critical review of the empirical evidence. *Transportation Research Part D: Transport and environment*, 17(7), 495–508.

Snijders, T., and Bosker, R. (1999). *Multilevel Analysis: An Introduction to Basic and Advanced Multilevel Modeling*. Sage Publications, Thousand Oaks, CA.

Chapter Five

Traffic Safety

The literature is replete with studies showing that areas with more residents, more employment, and more arterial lane miles experience more crashes (Levine et al. 1995a, 1995b; Hadayeghi et al. 2003; 2006; Kmet et al. 2003; Ladron de Guevara et al. 2004; Lovegrove and Sayed 2006). Such studies may be useful for crash prediction on individual facilities. However, they do not explain the crash rates on a per capita basis, only overall crash frequency on specific facilities or specific small areas. Where there are more people and jobs, there tends to be more of everything, from traffic to crime to coffee shops.

Given the direct relationship between vehicle miles traveled (VMT) and crash exposure, development patterns that generate lower VMT should also have lower traffic crash rates. If the relationship between VMT and traffic fatalities is near-linear, then sprawling communities, which are known to generate higher VMT per capita, should also report higher rates of traffic crashes and fatalities (Ewing et al. 2002).

Sprawl is partly characterized by strip commercial uses and out-sized big box retail outlets. Dumbaugh and Li (2011) examined many characteristics of the built environment and correlated them to the number of collisions involving pedestrians, cyclists, and motorists. They found major crash determinants include the total miles of arterial roadways and the presence of strip commercial uses and big box stores. However, pedestrian-scaled retail uses were associated with lower crash rates:

> Each additional mile of arterial thoroughfare was associated with a 9.3 percent increase in motorist-pedestrian crashes, each additional strip commercial use was associated with a 3 percent increase in vehicle-pedestrian

crashes, and each big box store was associated with an 8.7 percent increase in vehicle-pedestrian crashes.

(Dumbaugh and Li 2011)

Sprawl is also characterized by wide arterials, long blocks, and poor street connectivity. Marshall and Garrick (2011) analyzed 230,000 crashes occurring over 11 years in 24 cities in California to determine associations between crashes and street network characteristics, including street network density and street connectivity. Increasing street connectivity—normally associated with street grids—led to an increase in automobile crashes. The authors hypothesized that increased street connectivity leads to increased traffic conflicts and hence more crashes. However, the severity of crashes, and incidence of fatal crashes, were lower in downtown areas despite their grids. The authors argued that a decrease in fatal crashes is a result of lower vehicle speeds on streets in downtown areas.

In their 2003 article on sprawl vs. traffic fatalities, Ewing et al. (2003) found that for every 1 percent increase in the county compactness index, all-mode traffic fatality rates fell by 1.49 percent and pedestrian fatality rates fell by 1.47 percent, after adjusting for pedestrian exposure. In this chapter we seek to replicate these results using data for 2010. However, unlike the earlier study, we employ structural equation modeling, use a different database and dependent variables, include additional control variables, and test different compactness measures.

We would expect compact development patterns to produce fewer traffic accidents, injuries, and fatalities due to reduced vehicle miles driven and possibly also due to lower speeds of vehicle travel. We would also expect the relationship between sprawl and traffic fatalities to be more significant than in the original study due the larger sample of counties and greater variance in sprawl measures among these counties.

Methods

Data

There is no national source of crash data comparable to the Fatality Analysis Reporting System (FARS) database of fatalities. Instead, each state, through its department of transportation or department of public safety, maintains a comprehensive database of crashes that result in a vehicle being towed away, personal injury, or fatalities. Individual states establish their own reporting thresholds.

Traffic Safety

To test the theory that sprawl generates more crashes of all types, not just fatal crashes, we sought crash data from all 50 states. Crash data were obtained from all states via online databases or per an email/phone request. The survey years ranged from 2008 to 2011 with the majority from 2010 or 2011. The individual state crash data were compiled into a national database that includes 6 million crashes, nearly 1.8 million injury crashes, and nearly 30,000 fatal crashes.

Table 5.1: Crash Database

fips			All crashes	Injury crashes	Fatal crashes
1	Alabama	AL	124,258	26,943	814
2	Alaska	AK	12,462	3,659	51
4	Arizona	AZ	103,423	33,028	754
5	Arkansas	AR	59,076	17,759	509
6	California	CA	416,490	161,094	2,520
8	Colorado	CO	101,574	9,616	406
9	Connecticut	CT	101,625	25,391	299
10	Delaware	DE	20,872	5,204	97
12	Florida	FL	305,887	195,096	2,441
13	Georgia	GA	306,174	77,150	1,342
15	Hawaii	HI	7,940	4,816	108
16	Idaho	ID	21,410	8,036	163
17	Illinois	IL	281,878	60,057	835
18	Indiana	IN	181,452	31,413	726
19	Iowa	IA	54,804	16,957	386
20	Kansas	KS	59,740	13,325	354
21	Kentucky	KY	127,524	24,196	670
22	Louisiana	LA	34,467	34,007	460
23	Maine	ME	32,770	8,215	154
24	Maryland	MD	89,985	30,414	457
25	Massachusetts	MA	115,641	30,312	333
26	Michigan	MI	284,049	52,487	834
27	Minnesota	MN	72,117	21,662	334
28	Mississippi	MS	22,519	7,542	424
29	Missouri	MO	141,615	35,279	716
30	Montana	MT	19,747	5,352	192
31	Nebraska	NE	29,735	6,519	172
32	Nevada	NV	50,461	18,744	220
33	New Hampshire	NH	31,512	6,165	39

Table 5.1: Continued

fips			All crashes	Injury crashes	Fatal crashes
34	New Jersey	NJ	293,595	64,345	573
35	New Mexico	NM	46,156	13,120	319
36	New York	NY	439,660	131,131	1,097
37	North Carolina	NC	208,509	67,983	1,122
38	North Dakota	ND	18,823	3,548	130
39	Ohio	OH	296,170	73,427	941
40	Oklahoma	OK	68,701	23,683	462
41	Oregon	OR	49,053	23,887	310
42	Pennsylvania	PA	108,929	48,902	1,191
44	Rhode Island	RI	41,786	7,927	56
45	South Carolina	SC	107,673	31,152	700
46	South Dakota	SD	17,362	3,973	101
47	Tennessee	TN	195,799	48,293	903
48	Texas	TX	430,226	143,142	2,818
49	Utah	UT	46,272	14,153	217
50	Vermont	VT	10,279	1,862	57
51	Virginia	VA	211,054	43,072	644
53	Washington	WA	98,878	32,725	422
54	West Virginia	WV	29,946	9,050	166
55	Wisconsin	WI	112,516	28,965	515
56	Wyoming	WY	14,112	3,643	135
	Total		6,056,706	1,788,421	29,689

Variables

In this structural equation modeling (SEM) effort, we have four endogenous variables. County crash rates per 100,000 population were computed by dividing frequency counts by population in 100,000s obtained from the 2010 U.S. Census. The all-mode crash rates include all crashes involving private motor vehicles, buses, trains, taxis, bicycles, and pedestrians.

County VMT estimates were obtained from the Environmental Protection Agency (EPA). EPA has a process that uses surrogates such as population, roadway miles, and economic modeling to develop allocation factors for distributing the statewide total VMT to individual counties. Total VMT was divided by the number of households in each county in 2010 to obtain VMT per household. VMT per household is also treated as endogenous.

Traffic Safety

Exogenous variables came from various sources. From the 2010 Census, we downloaded data on population, households, gender, age, and race, and computed average household size, percentage of the population that is male, percentage of the population that is white, and percentage of the population of working age. Median household income for each county came from the 2010 American Community Survey (ACS), five-year estimates. The five-year estimates are based on data collected over a 60-month period from 2006 through 2010.

We also downloaded data on weather/climate and fuel price. Annual HDDs, CDDs, and annual precipitation data came from the NOAA's National Climatic Data Center for 2009 for HDD and 2010 for the other two variables. We recorded data for stations located in the same MSAs as the counties. In a few cases there were not weather stations in MSAs, so we used data from the closest station to a particular MSA. Gasoline price data at the MSA level were purchased from the OPIS. Retail prices are average prices from samples of stations in each MSA and are reported with all relevant taxes included. These prices are the true

Table 5.2: Variables (variables log transformed)

Variables		Data sources
Endogenous variables		
crash	traffic crash rate per 100,000 population	States, Census 2010
injury	injury crash rate per 100,000 population	States, Census 2010
fatal	fatal crash rate per 100,000 population	States, Census 2010
VMT	annual vehicle miles traveled per household	EPA 2011
Exogenous variables		
hhsize	average household size	Census 2010
pct1564	percentage of working age population (15–64 years old)	Census 2010
hhinc	median household income	ACS 2006–2010
white	percentage of white population	Census 2010
male	percentage of male population	Census 2010
fuel	average fuel price for the metropolitan area	OPIC database 2010
precip	annual precipitation (inches)	NOAA database 2010
hdd	heating degree-days	NOAA database 2010
cdd	cooling degree-days	NOAA database 2010
indexo	county compactness index for 2010 (using the same 2000 index variables)	
indexn	county compactness index for 2010 (including additional variables compared to 2000 index)	

Traffic Safety

posted "sign" prices (as they would appear outside a gas station). See Table 5.2 for the list of variables used in this chapter.

Method of Analysis

Models were estimated with structural equation modeling or SEM. SEM is a statistical methodology for evaluating complex hypotheses involving multiple, interacting variables (Grace 2006). SEM is a "model-centered" methodology that seeks to evaluate theoretically justified models against data. The SEM approach is based on the modern statistical view that theoretically based models, when they can be justified on scientific grounds, provide more useful interpretations than conventional methods that simply seek to reject the "null hypothesis" of no effect.

There are several related and distinctive features of SEM (Grace, 2006):

- Hypothesized path models are evaluated based on *a priori* knowledge about the processes under investigation using all available information.
- The investigator tests the degree to which the structure of one or more models is consistent with the structure inherent in the data. Many models that might be envisioned commonly are rejected because they are inconsistent with the data.
- Probability statements about the model are reversed from those associated with null hypotheses. Probability values (p-values) used in statistics are measures of the degree to which the data are unexpected, given the hypothesis being tested. In null hypothesis testing, a finding of a p-value <0.05 indicates that we can reject the null hypothesis because the data are very unlikely to come from a random process. In SEM, we seek a model that has a large p-value (>0.05) because that indicates that the data are not unlikely given that model (that is, the data are consistent with the model).
- Different processes operating in systems are distinguished by decomposing relationships into direct and indirect pathways. Pathways can, thus, be either simple or compound, depending on whether they pass through other variables or not. The total effect of one factor on another is the cumulative impact summed over all the pathways connecting the two factors.

The estimation of structural equation (SE) models involves solving a set of equations. There is an equation for each "response" or "endogenous" variable in the network. Variables that are solely predictors of other variables are termed "influences" or "exogenous" variables. Typically, solution procedures for SE

Traffic Safety

models focus on the observed versus model-implied correlations in the data. The unstandardized correlations or co-variances are the raw material for the analyses. Models are automatically compared to a "saturated" model (one that allows all variables to inter-correlate), and this comparison allows the analysis to discover missing pathways and, thereby, reject inconsistent models.

In this analysis, data first were examined for frequency distributions and simple bivariate relationships, especially for linearity. This suggested the need for data transformation. To equalize and stabilize variances, improve linearity, and still allow ready interpretations, all variables were log transformed.

Results

We have estimated three SE models with Amos 19.0, a popular SEM software package with a good graphic display. Maximum likelihood methods are used in the estimations. Model evaluation are based on four factors: (1) theoretical soundness; (2) chi-square tests of absolute model fit; (3) root-mean-square errors of approximation (RMSEA), which unlike the chi-square, correct for sample size; and (4) comparative fit indices (CFI).

The path diagram in Figure 5.1 is copied directly from Amos. Causal pathways are represented by straight uni-directional arrows. Correlations are represented by curved bi-directional arrows (to simplify the already complex causal diagram, some correlations are omitted). By convention, circles represent error terms in the model, of which there is one for each endogenous (response) variable.

The main goodness-of-fit measure used to choose among models is the chi-square statistic. In SEM, we seek a model with a small chi-square and large p-value (>0.05) because that indicates that the data are not unlikely given that model (that is, the data are consistent with the model).

The first analysis simply validates the findings of earlier analysis (Ewing et al. 2003). The main endogenous variable is the natural logarithm of the number of fatal crashes per 100,000 population. Another endogenous variable, the natural logarithm of VMT per household, is a mediating variable on the causal pathways between the exogenous variables and the fatal crash rate. The exogenous variables are as above.

Judged by its significant coefficients, low model chi-square, and sample-size adjusted fit (the RMSEA), the first model fits the data well. The comparative fit index (CFI) value shows that the model explains most of the total discrepancy in the data (>99%).

Direct effects are presented in Table 5.3. Most of the causal paths shown in the path diagram are statistically significant (have non-zero values). The

Traffic Safety

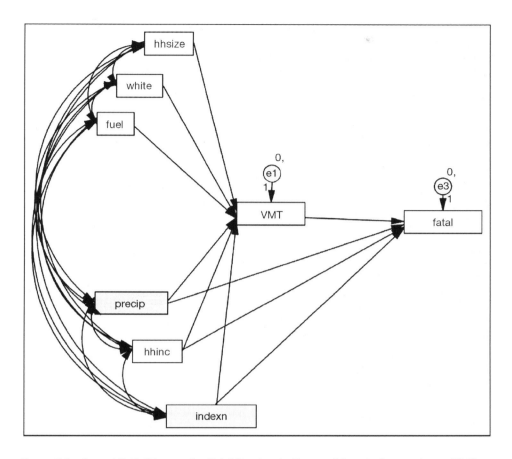

Figure 5.1: Causal Path Diagram for Fatal Crashes in Terms of County Compactness, VMT, and Other Variables

exceptions are a couple paths that are theoretically significant, though not statistically significant. Income and average household size are directly related to VMT, while the percentage of whites in the population, annual precipitation, and average fuel price are inversely related to VMT. Larger households have more complex activity patterns than do smaller households. Higher-income households own more cars, and consume more land at lower residential densities. Due to patterns of housing segregation, whites may live closer to work and other common destinations. Rain and snow may discourage long-distance travel. High fuel prices increase the generalized cost of travel, thereby depressing travel. County compactness is, naturally, inversely related to VMT because origins and destinations are closer together in a compact county.

Traffic Safety

Table 5.3: Direct Effects of Variables on One Another in the Fatal Crash Model (log-log form)

y		x	Model 1 (Original indices)				Model 2 (Refined indices)			
			coeff.	std. err.	critical ratio	p-value	coeff.	std. err.	critical ratio	p-value
VMT	<—	hhsize	0.56	0.13	4.31	<0.001	0.34	0.14	2.44	0.02
VMT	<—	hhinc	0.12	0.04	2.71	0.01	0.08	0.04	1.78	0.08
VMT	<—	white	−0.21	0.05	−4.56	<0.001	−0.15	0.05	−3.34	<0.001
VMT	<—	precip	−0.03	0.03	−1.22	0.22	−0.07	0.03	−2.71	0.01
VMT	<—	fuel	−0.89	0.20	−4.38	<0.001	−0.74	0.21	−3.48	<0.001
fatal	<—	hhinc	−0.95	0.07	−13.38	<0.001	−0.98	0.07	−14.21	<0.001
fatal	<—	precip	0.17	0.05	3.72	<0.001	0.12	0.05	2.65	0.01
fatal	<—	VMT	0.61	0.06	10.27	<0.001	0.55	0.06	9.32	<0.001
VMT	<—	indexo	−0.95	0.06	−17.05	<0.001				
fatal	<—	indexo	−0.91	0.10	−8.90	<0.001				
VMT	<—	indexn					−0.78	0.05	−15.84	<0.001
fatal	<—	indexn					−0.95	0.09	−10.94	<0.001
chi-square			10.5 degrees of freedom = 3 p-value = 0.015				5.45 degrees of freedom = 3 p-value = 0.142			
RMSEA			0.053 p-value = 0.38				0.03 p-value = 0.75			
CFI			0.995				0.998			

VMT is directly and significantly related to the fatal crash rate, as one would expect. This relationship completes indirect pathways between our exogenous variables and the fatal crash rate. Some exogenous variables also have direct, significant relationships to the fatal crash rate. Income is negatively related to the fatal crash rate, perhaps because higher income households drive more crashworthy vehicles. The amount of precipitation is directly related to the fatal crash rate, as rainy and snow conditions are known to be implicated in crashes. Finally, the compactness index is inversely related to the fatal crash rate, even after controlling for VMT. One possible explanation is that dense areas have lower travel speeds, which lead to less severe crashes. Considering both direct and indirect effects, the original compactness index has a greater effect on the fatal crash rate than does the new compactness index (see Tables 5.4 and 5.5).

Traffic Safety

Table 5.4: Direct, Indirect, and Total Effects of the Original Compactness Index and Other Variables on the Fatal Crash Rate

	hhsize	hhinc	white	precip	fuel	VMT	indexo
Direct effect	0	−0.953	0	0.169	0	0.614	−0.914
Indirect effect	0.345	0.073	−0.126	−0.019	−0.548	0	−0.581
Total effect	0.345	−0.881	−0.126	0.15	−0.548	0.614	−1.495

Table 5.5: Direct, Indirect, and Total Effects of the New Compactness Index and Other Variables on the Fatal Crash Rate

	hhsize	hhinc	white	precip	fuel	VMT	indexn
Direct effect	0	−0.983	0	0.119	0	0.549	−0.946
Indirect effect	0.185	0.043	−0.082	−0.039	−0.404	0	−0.429
Total effect	0.185	−0.94	−0.082	0.08	−0.404	0.549	−1.375

The original compactness index features density variables that may do more to depress vehicular travel and speed than do the other elements of the new sprawl index.

The next analysis tests whether sprawling areas have higher or lower total crash rates than do compact areas. Compact areas generate lower VMT and hence less crash exposure than sprawling areas. At the same time, compact areas may have more fender benders due to stop-and-go driving, even as they have fewer serious crashes due to lower travel speeds. So *a priori*, our only expectation is that the relationship between sprawl and crash rates will be weaker for total crashes than for fatal crashes.

Direct relationships between compactness indices and total crashes are different than they were for fatal crashes (see Table 5.6). The original compactness index is no longer significantly related to the crash rate, and the new compactness index actually has its sign reversed, now having a positive direct relationship to the crash rate. We can envision concentrations of activity with lots of stop–and–go traffic causing many nonfatal crashes. The new compactness index represents, in addition to density, other components of sprawl. Strong population and employment centers, in particular, seem to generate more crashes. However, considering both direct and indirect effects, the original compactness index has a strong negative relationship to the total crash rate due to the negative indirect effect through VMT, while the new compactness index has a slight positive relationship (see Tables 5.7 and 5.8).

Table 5.6: Direct Effects of Variables on One Another in the Total Crash Model (log-log form)

y		x	Model 1 (Original index)				Model 2 (New index)			
			coeff.	std. err.	critical ratio	p-value	coeff.	std. err.	critical ratio	p-value
VMT	<—	hhsize	0.56	0.13	4.31	<0.001	0.34	0.14	2.44	0.02
VMT	<—	hhinc	0.12	0.04	2.71	0.01	0.08	0.04	1.78	0.08
VMT	<—	white	−0.21	0.05	−4.56	<0.001	−0.15	0.05	−3.34	<0.001
VMT	<—	precip	−0.03	0.03	−1.22	0.22	−0.07	0.03	−2.71	0.01
VMT	<—	fuel	−0.89	0.20	−4.38	<0.001	−0.74	0.21	−3.48	<0.001
crash	<—	VMT	0.26	0.06	4.19	<0.001	0.31	0.06	5.13	<0.001
crash	<—	hhsize	−1.25	0.23	−5.36	<0.001	−1.14	0.24	−4.86	<0.001
crash	<—	hhinc	0.03	0.08	0.33	0.74	0.01	0.08	0.08	0.94
crash	<—	precip	0.09	0.05	1.90	0.06	0.11	0.05	2.37	0.018
VMT	<—	indexo	−0.95	0.06	−17.05	<0.001				
crash	<—	indexo	0.14	0.10	1.38	0.17				
VMT	<—	indexn					−0.78	0.05	−15.84	<0.001
crash	<—	indexn					0.28	0.09	3.13	0.002
chi-square			0.74				1.09			
			degrees of freedom = 2				degrees of freedom = 2			
			p-value = 0.96				p-value = 0.58			
RMSEA			>0.001				>0.001			
			p-value = 0.996				p-value = 0.924			
CFI			1				1			

Table 5.7: Direct, Indirect, and Total Effects of the Original Compactness Index and Other Variables on the Total Crash Rate

	hhsize	hhinc	white	precip	fuel	VMT	indexo
Direct effect	−1.25	0.025	0	0.089	0	0.258	0.143
Indirect effect	0.145	0.031	−0.053	−0.008	−0.23	0	−0.244
Total effect	−1.105	0.056	−0.053	0.081	−0.23	0.258	−0.101

Table 5.8: Direct, Indirect, and Total Effects of the New Compactness Index and Other Variables on the Total Crash Rate

	hhsize	hhinc	white	precip	fuel	VMT	indexn
Direct effect	−1.142	0.006	0	0.112	0	0.312	0.281
Indirect effect	0.105	0.024	−0.047	−0.022	−0.23	0	−0.244
Total effect	−1.037	0.031	−0.047	0.09	−0.23	0.312	0.037

Table 5.9: Direct Effects of Variables on One Another in the Non-fatal Injury Crash Model (log-log form)

		Model 1 (Original indices)				Model 2 (Refined indices)			
y	x	coeff.	std. err.	critical ratio	p-value	coeff.	std. err.	critical ratio	p-value
VMT <—	hhsize	0.56	0.13	4.31	<0.001	0.34	0.14	2.44	0.015
VMT <—	hhinc	0.12	0.04	2.71	0.007	0.08	0.04	1.78	0.075
VMT <—	white	−0.21	0.05	−4.56	<0.001	−0.15	0.05	−3.34	<0.001
VMT <—	precip	−0.03	0.03	−1.22	0.223	−0.07	0.03	−2.71	0.007
VMT <—	fuel	−0.89	0.20	−4.38	<0.001	−0.74	0.21	−3.48	<0.001
injury <—	hhsize	−0.60	0.19	−3.20	0.001	−0.56	0.19	−2.85	0.004
injury <—	hhinc	−0.22	0.06	−3.63	<0.001	−0.20	0.06	−3.28	0.001
injury <—	white	−0.34	0.07	−5.15	<0.001	−0.38	0.06	−5.94	<0.001
injury <—	precip	0.35	0.04	9.90	<0.001	0.36	0.04	9.92	<0.001
injury <—	VMT	0.24	0.05	5.12	<0.001	0.22	0.05	4.60	<0.001
VMT <—	indexo	−0.95	0.06	−17.05	<0.001				
injury <—	indexo	0.36	0.09	3.94	<0.001				
VMT <—	indexn					−0.78	0.05	−15.84	<0.001
injury <—	indexn					0.23	0.08	3.02	0.003
chi-square		0.061 degrees of freedom = 1 p-value = 0.80				0.091 degrees of freedom = 1 p-value = 0.76			
RMSEA		<0.001 p-value = 0.93				<0.001 p-value = 0.92			
CFI		1				1			

Traffic Safety

Table 5.10: Direct, Indirect, and Total Effects of the Original Compactness Index and Other Variables on the Non-fatal Injury Crash Rate

	hhsize	hhinc	white	precip	fuel	VMT	indexo
Direct effect	−0.603	−0.223	−0.335	0.354	0	0.243	0.355
Indirect effect	0.137	0.029	−0.05	−0.007	−0.217	0	−0.231
Total effect	−0.466	−0.194	−0.385	0.347	−0.217	0.243	0.124

Table 5.11: Direct, Indirect, and Total Effects of the New Compactness Index and Other Variables on the Non-fatal Injury Crash Rate

	hhsize	hhinc	white	precip	fuel	VMT	indexn
Direct effect	−0.555	−0.2	−0.376	0.364	0	0.217	0.23
Indirect effect	0.073	0.017	−0.032	−0.015	−0.159	0	−0.169
Total effect	−0.482	−0.183	−0.408	0.349	−0.159	0.217	0.061

The final analysis may be the most surprising. Nonfatal injury crash rates were modeled using the same set of exogenous and endogenous variables as above (see Figure 5.1). Compactness indices have positive signs and, in the case of the new compactness index, a significant relationship at the 0.05 level. The direct effects of compactness indices on the injury crash rate actually overwhelm the indirect effects through VMT, and the net effect is positive for both compactness indices. Due to the large number of such crashes in our sample, and the intuitively plausible results for fatal crashes, we do not view this result as spurious. Apparently the inherently large number of traffic conflicts in compact areas (mostly at intersections) result in more crashes of a serious nature but not so serious as to be fatal.

Limitations

The new sprawl measures have been tested against traffic crash data. As in 2003, we hypothesized that county compactness would be inversely related to the total traffic fatality rate. This is due to the lower vehicle miles traveled in a compact environment, and also possibly to the lower speeds of travel.

We confirmed this hypothesis. This study suggests that sprawl is a significant risk factor for traffic fatalities. The recognition of this relationship is key, as it adds traffic safety to the other health risks associated with urban sprawl, namely, obesity and air and water pollution. However, the strong relationships observed

Traffic Safety

for fatal crashes do not extend to injury crashes or to total crashes, including those with property damage.

This study has weaknesses. The study design is ecological in nature. It treats each county as a homogenous unit, and assigns to it a single fatality rate and compactness index, even though there are likely to be large differences within its borders. In certain circumstances, such as the study of behaviors antecedent to injury, the analysis may need to extend down to the individual level.

We recognize that the fatality data studied are based on place of crash, while the other data are based on place of residence, which may be different. To the extent that fatalities occur during the morning or evening commute, a (reassuring) bias towards the null may exist. In other words, because most commuters who cross county borders live in lower-density bedroom communities and work in higher-density central areas, the traffic fatality rate in urban counties would be inflated relative to the population living there. Using these databases, we could not determine the extent to which such bias, if any, exists. One solution would be to study the relationship at the (multi-county) metropolitan area level, but this would be at the expense of desired precision in the measurement of differences within metropolitan areas.

Additional studies are needed to confirm these findings and extend our knowledge in key areas. An exploration of the relationship between vehicle speed, fatality rates, and specific street design features common to urban sprawl (e.g., wide, long streets) would help guide countermeasures.

References

Dumbaugh, E., and Li, W. (2011). Designing for the safety of pedestrians, cyclists, and motorists in the built environment. *Journal of the American Planning Association*, 77(1), 69–88.

Ewing, R., Schieber, R. A., and Zegeer, C.V. (2003). Urban sprawl as a risk factor in motor vehicle occupant and pedestrian fatalities. *American Journal of Public Health*, 93(9), 1541–1545.

Ewing, R., Schmid, T., Killingsworth, R., Zlot, A., and Raudenbush, S. (2003). Relationship between urban sprawl and physical activity, obesity, and morbidity. *American Journal of Health Promotion*, 18, 47–57.

Grace, J.B. (2006) *Structural Equation Modeling and Natural Systems*, Cambridge University Press, Cambridge.

Hadayeghi, A., Shalaby, A.S., and Persaud, B.N. (2003). Macro level accident prediction models for evaluating safety of urban transportation systems. *Trans-*

portation Research Record: Journal of the Transportation Research Board, 1840, 87–95.

Hadayeghi, A., Shalaby, A.S., Persaud, B.N., and Cheung, C. (2006). Temporal transferability and updating of zonal level accident prediction models. *Accident Analysis and Prevention*, 38(3), 579–589.

Kmet, L., Brasher, P., and Macarthur, C. (2003). A small area study of motor vehicle crash fatalities in Alberta, Canada. *Accident Analysis and Prevention*, 35(2), 177–182.

Ladron de Guevara, F., Washington, S.P., and Oh, J. (2004). Forecasting travel crashes at the planning levels: Simultaneous negative binomial crash model applied in Tucson, Arizona. *Transportation Research Record: Journal of the Transportation Research Board*, 1897, 191–199.

Levine, N., Kim, K.E., and Nitz, L.H. (1995a). Spatial analysis of Honolulu motor vehicle crashes: I. Spatial analysis. *Accident Analysis and Prevention*, 27(5), 663–674.

Levine, N., Kim, K.E., and Nitz, L.H. (1995b). Spatial analysis of Honolulu motor vehicle crashes: II. Zonal generators. *Accident Analysis and Prevention*, 27(5), 675–685.

Lovegrove, G.R., and Sayed, T. (2006). Macro-level collision prediction models for evaluating neighborhood traffic safety. *Canadian Journal of Civil Engineering*, 33(5), 609–621.

Marshall, W.E., and Garrick, N.W. (2011). Does street network design affect traffic safety? *Accident Analysis and Prevention*, 43(3), 769–781.

Chapter Six

Public Health

Obesity is a significant health problem and the prevalence of adult obesity and overweight in the U.S. has risen significantly in the last 30 years (Khan et al. 2009). The rising incidence of obesity presents serious long-term challenges including decreased life expectancy and the potential for negative impacts on an individual's quality of life, the availability and cost of future health care, and the viability and productivity of future generations. There are many influences on weight and health including genetics, socioeconomic status, race/ethnicity, gender, access to food, levels of physical activity, and neighborhood environments. The fundamental cause of obesity and overweight is an imbalance between calories consumed and calories expended and the two main modifiable risk factors are unhealthy diets and physical inactivity (Black and Macinko 2008; Trost et al. 2001; 2002).

It is commonly recognized that even a moderate amount of physical activity can result in significant health benefits, yet current research indicates that physical activity levels have declined with many adults (43 percent) failing to meet the recommended physical activity requirements (Trogdon et al. 2008). In the last 50 years activity levels have dropped for a variety of reasons including new technologies and automation that make our lives easier, television and computer use that lead to sedentary life styles, automobile use that substitutes for active travel, and urban sprawl that all but guarantees automobile dependence (Committee on Physical Activity 2005). Research indicates that the built environment is associated with active travel and leisure time physical activity in adults (Goldstein 2011; Wong et al. 2011).

Walking is the most common form of physical activity (Lee and Moudon 2004). Availability and access to recreational facilities, high residential densities, mixed land uses, perceived safety, and aesthetics are most often associated with

Public Health

physical activity (Durand et al. 2011; Humpel et al. 2002; Kaczynski and Henderson 2007; McCormack et al. 2004; Owen et al. 2004; Trost et al. 2002; Vancauwenberg et al. 2011).

Socioeconomic factors as well as characteristics of the built environment may also restrict access to healthy foods. All are components of an "ecological" approach to obesity research. This ecological approach to research is a common thread throughout the body of research investigating the influences of dietary intake, physical activity, socioeconomic, and demographic variables as they relate to obesity (Galvez et al. 2010).

In 2003, Ewing et al. (2003) published a landmark study that established a relationship between health behaviors, health outcomes, and the county sprawl index and became the most widely cited academic paper in the social sciences as of late 2005, according to *Essential Science Indicators* (Reuters).[1] After controlling for age, education, fruit and vegetable consumption, and other socio-demographic and behavioral covariates, they found that adults living in sprawling counties had higher body mass indices (BMIs) and were more likely to be obese (BMI >30) than were their counterparts living in compact counties.

In the years since this original study was published, there has been a plethora of research studies in both planning and public health investigating the unique relationship between the built environment and health outcomes. A recent meta-study identified 36 literature reviews: 26 with physical activity as the outcome variable, 5 focused on obesity, and an additional 5 covering both. Youth were the focus of 11 studies, 7 focused on either adults or seniors, and 17 did not specify age groups (Ding and Gebel 2012).

An additional search of published research studies (conducted in May 2011) resulted in a total inventory of 82 articles that relate some dimension of the built environment to obesity. Most studies focused on adults (53), were cross sectional in research design (73), and addressed the built environment at the neighborhood scale (65). One study included built environmental variables at both the meso (neighborhood) and macro (county) scales (Joshu et al. 2008). This growing body of research suggests that some built environments may be more "obesogenic" than others through influences on dietary intake and physical inactivity (Black and Macinko 2008).

Even more recently, the amount of multidisciplinary research on obesity and the built environment has grown at a frenzied pace. There are now multiple reviews of the reviews summarizing literally hundreds of articles. A recent literature review uncovered 5,642 articles on the subject (Mackenbach et al. 2014). The reviewers selected a random sample of 500 titles and abstracts, and further narrowed the sample to 212 full articles that were read by the first two authors of the review. Of these articles, 92 were included in the final literature review. We concur with the conclusion:

> With the exception of urban sprawl and land use mix in the U.S. the results of the current review confirm that the available research does not allow robust identification of ways in which the physical environment influences adult weight status, even after taking into account methodological quality.
>
> (Mackenbach et al. 2014)

Of the 20 studies published between 2003 and 2007, 17 established statistically significant links between some aspect of the built environment and obesity (Papas et al. 2007), and correlations between sprawl and obesity have been affirmed (Frank et al. 2004; Kelly-Schwartz et al. 2004; Lopez 2004; Sturm and Cohen 2004; Committee on Physical Activity 2005; Cho et al. 2006; Doyle et al. 2006; Ewing et al. 2006; Joshu et al. 2008, Mackenbach et al. 2014).

As with the land use–travel literature, the possibility of self-selection has been raised in this literature as well. Two studies have garnered media attention by contending that residential self-selection, not environmental determinism, accounts for the relationship between sprawl and obesity (Plantinga and Bernell 2007; Eid et al. 2008). Both conclude that people with higher BMIs choose to live in sprawling neighborhoods. One can understand indifference to the built environment on the part of overweight individuals, but actual preference for places that preclude physical activity, when these people don't plan to engage in it anyway, defies logic.

Methods

This chapter updates the work of Ewing et al. (2003). We model multiple health outcomes and behaviors in terms of the updated and refined compactness/sprawl measures presented above, plus appropriate control variables.

Geographic Scale

This study represents the built environment at the county scale rather than the smaller neighborhood scale. The main reason is expediency, since the health database used in this study, for reasons of confidentiality, only supplies geocodes for respondents by county. For the same reason, the earliest studies of the built environment and obesity also represented the built environment with county or metropolitan metrics.

Public Health

Since then, most studies have chosen instead to characterize the built environments of individuals at the neighborhood scale, whether in terms of census tracts, block groups, or small buffers around individuals' homes. There has been an implicit assumption that walking distance from home is the operative scale at which the built environment affects physical activity, food availability, and ultimately weight. This is just an assumption. Adults spend most of their waking hours away from home. Something like 30 to 40 percent of all trips are made from one place to another other than home.

The average trip length in the U.S., according to the National Household Travel Survey of 2009, is almost 10 miles, which takes the traveler well beyond the bounds of the neighborhood. Even trips to buy goods and services, the shortest trips, average about five miles. Judged by the length of trips for grocery shopping and eating out, the relevant food environment for an American is at least five miles from home. The relevant recreational environment is at least 10 miles from home.

A sprawling built environment produces long trips by automobile, which cut into time available for leisure activities. There may be simply less time available for any kind of physical activity for Americans living in sprawl.

To our knowledge, only one study has compared the power of neighborhood and county environments as predictors of obesity (Joshu et al. 2008). While this study found that perceived neighborhood characteristics were more important than objectively measured county characteristics, the jury is still out on the appropriate scale for such research.

Data and Variables

Our health-related data come from the Behavioral Risk Factor Surveillance System (BRFSS), a telephone survey conducted by state health departments and managed by the Centers for Disease Control and Prevention (CDC). Over 350,000 adults are interviewed nationally each year to collect detailed information on health risk behaviors, preventive health practices, and health care access primarily related to chronic disease and injury.

We use a subsample of individuals for which county geocodes of residence are available for public use. Our data come from the Selected Metropolitan/Micropolitan Area Risk Trends (SMART) project, which is populated with BRFSS data for metropolitan and micropolitan statistical areas with 500 or more respondents. We have included data for survey years 2007 through 2010 (see Table 6.1 for a list of variables). Different questions are asked in different survey years (all four years for most variables

Public Health

but only two years for some). This accounts for the different sample sizes for different variables.

Our health outcome variables fall into three categories: weight status, physical activity, and chronic diseases. Weight status variables are calculated from self-reported height and weight. BMI is a continuous variable defined as weight in kilograms divided by height in meters squared (kg/m^2). Obesity status is dichotomous, defined as having a BMI greater than or equal to 30.0. One physical activity outcome is dichotomous: whether a respondent reported "any physical activity" in the last month. A second is continuous: minutes of moderate physical activity per week, which includes the kind of walking we expect to see in compact areas. Chronic disease outcomes are the status conditions of hypertension, diabetes, and coronary heart disease as diagnosed by a health care professional and reported by the respondent.

Gender, age, race/ethnicity, income, and educational attainment are included as control variables representing individual-level sociodemographics. The reference groups for these variables are females, white non–Hispanics, college graduates, persons aged 18 to 30 years, and households with income US$75,000 or greater. Smoking status and fruit and vegetable consumption are also included as control variables representing individual health behaviors. The control variables have very predictable results both within and between models. They are summarized in this chapter. Complete results are presented on the NIH website.

Individual respondents are nested within counties and hence share the characteristics of the county built, social, and natural environments. Having individuals nested within counties, this dataset violates the independence assumption of OLS, and instead is analyzed using multi-level modeling and HLM 6.08. Hierarchical linear modeling is applied to the continuous outcomes (BMI and minutes of moderate physical activity per week), while hierarchical nonlinear modeling (logistic modeling) is applied to the dichotomous outcomes (all other outcome variables).

The variables of particular interest are the compactness measures: original county compactness index, new county compactness index, and county density, mix, centering, and street factors. The control variables are precipitation, heating degree days, cooling degree days, and the violent crime rate, all for year 2010.

We introduce a new variable into this analysis, to test for significant relation-ships to physical activity: percentage of land area of the county occupied by parks, excluding rural census tracts. Low densities, large blocks, segregated land uses, and weak centers all translate into poor accessibility. To get at another

Public Health

dimension of sprawl, lack of functional open space, we needed a different approach and data source. The open space metric was produced using data created by Tele Atlas North America, Inc. and provided under license to ESRI for inclusion in ESRI Data & Maps for use with ESRI® software. The data were created for 2010 using ESRI ArcMap 10.0. U.S. Parks is a SDC Feature Database containing thousands of polygons representing national, state, county, regional, and local–level parks. For our current work, the dataset was filtered to remove national and state parks as well as golf courses. Census geography (2010) for U.S. counties was connected with the park dataset using the "union" tool within ArcMap. As before, rural census tracts with fewer than 100 persons per square mile were excluded. Multiple park polygons were then aggregated resulting in total park land area in square miles.

Table 6.1: BRFSS Variables and Sample Sizes

Variables		Scale	n
Level 1 dependent variables			
bmi	body mass index	continuous	675,784
obese	obese status	dichotomous	676,524
anypa	any physical exercise in last 30 days	dichotomous	709,099
minmod	minutes of moderate physical activity per week	continuous	159,965
bphigh	diagnosed high blood pressure	dichotomous	354,826
chd	diagnosed heart disease	dichotomous	703,942
diabetes	diagnosed diabetes	dichotomous	709,234
Level 1 independent variables			
male	male	dichotomous	709,889
age3044	age 30–44	dichotomous	709,889
age4564	age 45–64	dichotomous	709,889
age6574	age 65–74	dichotomous	709,889
age75+	age 75+	dichotomous	709,889
black	black non-Hispanic	dichotomous	701,572
otherrace	other non-Hispanic	dichotomous	701,394
Hispanic	Hispanic	dichotomous	701,572
lesshs	less than high school	dichotomous	709,889
hsgrad	high school graduate	dichotomous	709,889
somecoll	some college	dichotomous	709,889
inclt25	income <$25,000	dichotomous	709,889

Public Health

Table 6.1: Continued

Variables		Scale	n
inc2550	income $25,000-$50,000	dichotomous	615,801
inc5075	income $50,000-$75,000	dichotomous	615,801
smoke	current smoker	dichotomous	705,549
recfv	recommended servings fruits/vegetables	dichotomous	343,695
Level 2 independent variables			
crime	violent crime rate per 100,000 population	continuous	316
precip	annual precipitation	continuous	316
hhd	annual heating degree days	continuous	316
cdd	annual cooling degree days	continuous	316
park	percentage park land (relative to total land area)	continuous	316
indexo	county compactness index for 2010 (using the same 2000 index variables)	continuous	316
indexn	county compactness index for 2010 (including additional variables compared to 2000 index)	continuous	316
denfac	density factor (a weighted combination of 5 density variables)	continuous	316
mixfac	mix factor (a weighted combination of 3 mixed-use variables)	continuous	316
cenfac	centering factor (a weighted combination of 4 centering variables)	continuous	316
strfac	street factor (a weighted combination of 4 street-related variables)	continuous	316

BMI and Obesity

BMI data are available for all four survey years. BMI is higher for males than females and for black non-Hispanics and Hispanics than white non-Hispanics. BMI is lower for other non-Hispanics than whites, the former being mostly Asian. BMI is higher for those with less education, though the pattern is complicated. BMI increases with age until age 65, when it begins to decline. BMI declines with income following a smooth curve. BMI is lower for those who smoke and those who meet the recommended servings of five fruit or vegetables a day. BMI is lower in counties with more land devoted to parks, and higher in counties with more HDDs. In both cases, there is a logical connection to physical activity.

Public Health

As for the variables of greatest interest, those related to the built environment, BMI is strongly and negatively related to the original and new compactness indices (see Table 6.2). The new compactness index has a slightly stronger relationship to BMI and a slightly higher significance level. By either measure, controlling for sociodemographic and behavioral covariates, residents of more compact counties have lower BMIs. Of the four individual compactness factors, three have the expected negative signs and the fourth, the streets factor, has no relationship. The most significant influence is the mix factor (significant at the 0.001 level), followed by the density factor (significant at the 0.049 level). Comparatively, compactness measures have much higher significance levels in this study than in the 2003 study (Ewing et al. 2003). This is not due to the sample size. There are actually fewer counties represented in the 2010 sample. Perhaps the reason for the added significance is the limitation of this sample to larger and more urban counties with a minimum of 500 respondents. The earlier sample included some counties that are much smaller and less urban.

As with BMI, males, black non–Hispanics, and Hispanics have higher probabilities of being obese than their reference categories (see NIH website). The likelihood of obesity declines with income and generally with education. Obesity is less prevalent among current smokers and those who consume the recommended servings of fruits and vegetables. In all models, the likelihood of obesity is higher for residents of counties with more HDDs. In two models, prevalence of obesity is higher in counties with more violent crime. In another, the prevalence of obesity is lower in counties with more park space. There are logical connections to physical activity.

Controlling for covariates, the original and new compactness indices are strongly and negatively related obesity, with the new index having a slightly stronger relationship (see Table 6.3). In the more fully specified model, the mix and density factors are negatively related to obesity status, in that order of significance. The centering and street factors are not significant.

Physical Activity

We modeled two physical activity (PA) variables in this study (Tables 6.4 and 6.5). The first PA variable indicates whether a respondent engaged in any physical activity in the last month. The question reads: "During the past month, other than your regular job, did you participate in any physical activities or exercises such as running, calisthenics, golf, gardening, or walking for exercise?" This question is included in all four years of the BRFSS survey.

Table 6.2: Relationships to BMI (with robust standard errors)

	Model 1			Model 2			Model 3		
	coeff.	t–ratio	p-value	coeff.	t-ratio	p-value	coeff.	t-ratio	p-value
Constant	25.14	95.14	<0.001	25.13	101.01	<0.001			
indexo	−0.00897	−4.25	<0.001						
indexn				−0.00910	−4.50	<0.001			
denfac							−0.0066	−1.98	0.049
mixfac							−0.0117	−3.33	0.001
cenfac							−0.00085	−0.48	0.633
strfac							0.0033	1.43	0.153
psuedo-R2	0.079			0.079			0.080		

Public Health

Table 6.3: Relationships to Obesity (with robust standard errors)

	Model 1			Model 2			Model 3		
	coeff.	t-ratio	p-value	coeff.	t-ratio	p-value	coeff.	t-ratio	p-value
Constant	−1.68	−19.58	<0.001	−1.66	−19.65	<0.001			
indexo	−0.0035	−4.75	<0.001						
indexn				−0.00401	−6.11	<0.001			
denfac							−0.0028	−2.29	0.023
mixfac							−0.0036	−2.53	0.012
cenfac							−0.00075	−0.93	0.351
strfac							0.0013	1.17	0.243
psuedo R2	0.50			0.57			0.58		

Males are more likely to be physically active than females. The likelihood of any physical activity generally increases with education and income, and declines with age. The two compactness indices are not significantly related to engaging in any physical activity. This result parallels that of the 2003 study (Ewing et al. 2003).

It is not clear from the phrasing of the BRFSS question whether active travel (walking or bicycling to a destination) is covered and will be captured by this variable. Thus it is possible that respondents walk or bike more in compact areas but simply do not report it as exercise.

Results are mixed for the four individual factors. The degree of centering and the mix factor have a positive relationship to physical activity, while density has a negative relationship. Assuming these results aren't spurious, their counter-vailing effects may explain the lack of significance of the overall compactness indices.

The second physical activity variable is a calculated value for minutes of moderate physical activity per week. The 2003 study found that minutes of leisure-time walking were positively related to county compactness (Ewing et al. 2003). This was the only physical activity variable with a significant relationship to compactness. More recent surveys have not asked about specific physical activities such as walking and bicycling, but instead have asked about moderate and vigorous physical activity generally. If any relationship is likely to show up between compactness and physical activity, it will be in minutes of moderate activity.

In BRFSS 2007 and 2009, respondents were asked if they engaged in moderate physical activities outside work for at least 10 minutes at a time.

Public Health

Table 6.4: Relationships to Any Physical Activity (with robust standard errors)

	Model 1			Model 2			Model 3		
	coeff.	t-ratio	p-value	coeff.	t-ratio	p-value	coeff.	t-ratio	p-value
Constant	2.80	33.41	<0.001	2.71	32.33	<0.001			
indexo	0.000012	0.021	0.988						
indexn				0.00079	1.41	0.160			
denfac							−0.0019	−1.94	0.053
mixfac							0.0017	1.69	0.091
cenfac							0.0016	2.60	0.010
strfac							0.00033	0.35	0.726
psuedo R2	0.67			0.67			0.70		

The specific question included in the 2007 and 2009 surveys was:

> We are interested in two types of physical activity: vigorous and moderate. Vigorous activities cause large increases in breathing or heart rate while moderate activities cause small increases in breathing or heart rate. Now, thinking about the moderate activities you do when you are not working (if employed) in a usual week, do you do moderate activities for at least 10 minutes at a time, such as brisk walking, bicycling, vacuuming, gardening, or anything else that causes some increase in breathing or heart rate?

If the answer was "yes," follow-up questions were asked about amounts of physical activity. Some of the values provided were unrealistically high. Therefore, values were truncated at 1,260 minutes a week, which represents three hours per day seven days a week and included 99 percent of all respondents.

Results are similar to those for the other PA variable, except that respondents with less education get more moderate physical activity than those with college degrees. As one might expect, moderate physical activity is negatively related to precipitation, HDDs, and CDDs, these environmental conditions apparently discouraging outside activities. Surprisingly, after controlling for other variables, moderate physical activity appears to be negatively related to county compactness. We can think of no obvious explanation for these results, but would note that very little of the variance in our dataset is explained by these models. In a Bayesian statistical sense, this one result does not negate all contrary evidence.

Public Health

Table 6.5: Relationships to Minutes of Moderate Physical Activity per Week (with robust standard errors)

	Model 1			Model 2			Model 3		
	coeff.	t-ratio	p-value	coeff.	t-ratio	p-value	coeff.	t-ratio	p-value
Constant	268.34	32.35	<0.001	269.40	28.90	<0.001			
indexo	−0.14	−2.432	0.016						
indexn				−0.154	−2.460	0.015			
denfac							0.046	0.54	0.592
mixfac							−0.090	−0.68	0.500
cenfac							−0.050	−0.69	0.493
strfac							−0.042	−0.36	0.723
psuedo R2	0.16			0.16			0.17		

Chronic Diseases

Three health outcomes were modeled in this study: the diagnosed conditions of high blood pressure, heart disease, and diabetes (Tables 6.6 through 6.8). These are known to be related to obesity and physical inactivity, and the former at least is related to sprawl. However, these three chronic conditions are "downstream" outcomes of obesity and physical inactivity, and highly dependent on diet and heredity. Thus, *a priori*, we cannot say whether they will have a relationship to the urban sprawl.

Table 6.6: Relationships to High Blood Pressure (with robust standard errors)

	Model 1			Model 2			Model 3		
	coeff.	t-ratio	p-value	coeff.	t-ratio	p-value	coeff.	t-ratio	p-value
Constant	−2.87	−37.11	<0.001	−2.83	−37.14	<0.001			
indexo	−0.0018	−3.15	0.002						
indexn				−0.0021	−3.62	0.001			
denfac							−0.00068	−0.73	0.463
mixfac							−0.0011	−1.25	0.214
cenfac							−0.00044	−0.74	0.462
strfac							−0.00047	−0.53	0.595
Psuedo R2	0.54			0.55			0.57		

Public Health

Table 6.7: Relationships to Coronary Heart Disease (with robust standard errors)

	Model 1			Model 2			Model 3		
	coeff.	t-ratio	p-value	coeff.	t-ratio	p-value	coeff.	t-ratio	p-value
Constant	−6.01	−20.86	<0.001	−5.96	−20.73	<0.001			
indexo	−0.0024	−1.79	0.073						
indexn				−0.0028	−2.12	0.034			
denfac							−0.0014	−0.67	0.504
mixfac							−0.0058	−3.07	0.003
cenfac							−0.0013	−1.35	0.179
strfac							0.0025	1.61	0.107
Psuedo R2	0.51			0.58			0.61		

Table 6.8: Relationships to Diabetes (with robust standard errors)

	Model 1			Model 2			Model 3		
	coeff.	t-ratio	p-value	coeff.	t-ratio	p-value	coeff.	t-ratio	p-value
Constant	−5.18	−40.74	<0.001	−5.17	−40.10	<0.001			
indexo	−0.0015	−2.22	0.034						
indexn				−0.0016	−2.27	0.024			
denfac							−0.00087	−0.73	0.464
mixfac							−0.0033	−2.46	0.015
cenfac							−0.00024	−0.36	0.714
strfac							0.0011	0.97	0.331
Psuedo R2	0.57			0.58			0.60		

Largely tracking the findings for obesity, the incidence of diabetes, heart disease, and high blood pressure increases with age, declines with income, and declines with education. All three conditions are more prevalent in males than females. The effect of race is mixed.

More interestingly, the two overall compactness indices are negatively associated with all three chronic diseases. The new compactness index has slightly stronger relationships to these conditions than does the original compactness index. The mix factor is the most significantly related of the individual factors with a negative relationship to chronic disease.

Public Health

Limitations

The new sprawl measures have been tested against physical activity, obesity, and chronic disease data from BRFSS. We hypothesized that county compactness would be inversely related to moderate physical activity, BMI, obesity, hypertension, diabetes, and coronary heart disease (after controlling for relevant covariates). With the exception of physical activity, these relationships have been confirmed.

This analysis is subject to important limitations that call for additional research:

- Because this study is ecological and cross sectional in nature, we cannot say that sprawl causes obesity, high blood pressure, or any other health condition. Our study simply indicates that sprawl is associated with these conditions. Future research using longitudinal data is needed to tackle the more difficult job of testing for causality.
- The presumptive relationships between sprawl and health are multiple and complex. In particular, leisure time physical activity constitutes only one of four major sources of physical activity. Greater precision in characterizing physical activity will help disentangle the effects of sprawl on health.
- We recognize that the relationships between sprawl and behavior or weight are probably not completely linear. It may be that certain thresholds or critical levels of "compactness" are needed before community design begins to have a palpable influence on physical activity—increasing density from one or two houses per acre to three or four may not meet the threshold needed for change.
- This study relates health to the built environment at the county scale, which is large compared to the living and working environments of most residents. Geocodes are only available from BRFSS down to the county level. If environmental effects are felt most strongly at the community or neighborhood scale, these results may understate the effects of the built environment on health.
- Because they are not directly measured in any of the compactness/sprawl measures, this study does not account for many other environmental variables that may act directly or interact to influence physical activity and hence health such as sidewalks and topography.
- People who have specific residential preferences may self-select to live in walkable or, alternatively, auto-dominant environments rather than

Public Health

environments themselves affecting physical activity and hence weight. The direction of causality cannot be determined from a cross sectional database like that used in this chapter. However, the weight of evidence from the built environment-travel literature indicates that the environment affects travel choices independent of residential preferences, and that environmental effects are stronger than self-selection effects (Ewing and Cervero 2010).

- By focusing on physical activity, this study largely ignores the other side of the energy equation, calories consumed as opposed to calories expended. Only our fruit and vegetable consumption variable begins to get at that dimension of the problem. Caloric intake may have a spatial component. Future research could, for example, relate the density of fast food restaurants and availability of food choices to diet and obesity.

Note

1   See http://wokinfo.com/products_tools/analytical/essentialscience indicators/.

References

Black, J.L., and Macinko, J. (2008). Neighborhoods and obesity. *Nutrition Reviews*, 66(1), 2–20.

Cho, S., Chen, Z., Yen, S.T., and Eastwood, D.B. (2006). *The Effects of Urban Sprawl on Body Mass Index: Where People Live Does Matter.* The 52nd Annual ACCI Conference, Baltimore, Maryland, March 15–18.

Committee on Physical Activity, Transportation, and Land Use. (2005). *Does the Built Environment Influence Physical Activity? Examining the Evidence: Special Report 282.* Transportation Research Board Institute of Medicine.

Ding, D., and Gebel, K.M. (2012). Built environment, physical activity, and obesity: What have we learned from reviewing the literature? *Health & Place*, 18, 100–105.

Doyle, S., Kelly-Schwartz, A., Schlossberg, M., and Stockard, J. (2006). Active community environments and health: The relationship of walkable and safe communities to individual health. *Journal of the American Planning Association*, 72(1), 19–31.

Durand, C.P., Andalib, M., Dunton, G.F., Wolch, J., and Pentz, M.A. (2011). A systematic review of built environment factors related to physical activity and obesity risk: Implications for smart growth urban planning. *Obesity Reviews*, 12, 173–182.

Eid, J., Overman, H.G., and Puga, D., and Turner, Matthew, A. (2008) Fat city: Questioning the relationship between urban sprawl and obesity. *Journal of Urban Economics*, 63(2), 385–404.

Ewing, R., Cervero, R. (2010). Travel and the built environment: A meta-analysis. *Journal of the American Planning Association*, 76(3), 265–294.

Ewing R., Schmid, T., Killingsworth, R., Zlot, A., and Raudenbush, S. (2003). Relationship between urban sprawl and physical activity, obesity, and morbidity. *American Journal of Health Promotion*, 18, 47–57.

Ewing, R., Brownson, R., and Berrigan, D. (2006). Relationship between urban sprawl and weight of U.S. youth. *American Journal of Preventive Medicine*, 31, 464–474.

Frank, L.D., Andresen, M.A., and Schmid, T.L. (2004). Obesity relationships with community design, physical activity, and time spent in cars. *American Journal of Preventive Medicine*, 27(2), 87–96.

Frenkel, A., and Ashkenazi, M. (2008). Measuring urban sprawl: How can we deal with it? *Environment and Planning B: Planning and Design*, 35(1), 56–79.

Galvez, M.P., Meghan, P., and Yen, I. (2010). Childhood obesity and the built environment: A review of the literature from 2008–2009. *Current Opinion in Pediatrics*, 22(2), 202–207.

Goldstein, H. (2011). *Multilevel Statistical Models*. Wiley Series in Probability and Statistics, Wiley, West Sussex.

Humpel, N., Owen, N., and Leslie, E. (2002). Environmental factors associated with adults' participation in physical activity. *American Journal of Preventive Medicine*, 26, 119–125.

Joshu, C.E., Boehmer, T.K., Brownson, R.C., and Ewing, R. (2008). Personal, neighbourhood and urban factors associated with obesity in the United States. *Journal of Epidemiology and community Health*, 62, 202–208.

Kaczynski, A.T., and Henderson, K.A. (2007). Environmental correlates of physical activity: A review of evidence about parks and recreation. *Leisure Sciences*, 29, 315–354.

Kelly-Schwartz, A., Stockard, J., Doyle, S., and Schlossberg, M. (2004). Is sprawl unhealthy? A multilevel analysis of the relationship of metropolitan sprawl to the health of individuals. *Journal of Planning Education and Research*, 24, 184–196.

Khan, L.K., Sobush, K., Keener, D., Goodman, K., Lowry, A., Kakietek, J., and Zaro, S. (2009). Centers for disease control and prevention. Recommended community strategies and measurements to prevent obesity in the United States. *Morbidity and Mortality Weekly Report*, 58(RR-7), 1–29.

Lee, C., and Moudon, A.V. (2004). Physical activity and environment research in the health field: Implications for urban and transportation planning practice and research. *Journal of Planning Literature*, 19(2), 147–181.

Lopez, R. (2004). Urban sprawl and risk for being overweight or obese. *American Journal of Public Health*, 94(9), 1574–1579.

Lopez, R., and Hynes, H.P. (2003). Sprawl in the 1990s: Measurement, distribution, and trends. *Urban Affairs Review*, 38(3), 325–355.

Mackenbach, J.D., Rutter, H., Compernolle, S., Glonti, K., Oppert, J.M., Charreire H., ... and Lakerveld, J. (2014). Obesogenic environments: A systematic review of the association between the physical environment and adult weight status, the SPOTLIGHT project. *BMC Public Health*, 14(1), 233.

McCormack, G., Giles-Corti, B., Lange, A., Smith, T., Martin, K., and Pikora, T. (2004). An update of recent evidence of the relationship between objective and self-report measures of the physical environment and physical activity behaviours. *Journal of Science and Medicine in Sport*, 7(1), 81–92.

Owen, N.P., Humpel, N.P., Leslie, E.P., Bauman, A.P., and Sallis, J.F.P. (2004). Understanding environmental influences on walking review and research agenda. *American Journal of Preventative Medicine*, 27(1), 67–76.

Papas, M.A., Alberg, A.J., Ewing, R., Helzlsouer, K.J., Gary, T.L., and Klassen, A. (2007). The built environment and obesity. *Epidemiologic Reviews*, 29(1), 129–143.

Plantinga, A., and Bernell, S. (2007). The association between urban sprawl and obesity: Is it a two-way street? *Journal of Regional Science*, 47(5), 857–879.

Sturm, R., and Cohen, D. (2004). Suburban sprawl and physical and mental health, *Public Health*, 118(7), 488–496.

Trogdon, J.G., Finkelstein, E.A., Hylands, T., Dellea, P.S., and Kamal-Bahl, A.S.J. (2008). Indirect costs of obesity: A review of the current literature. *Obesity Review*, 9, 489–500.

Trost, S., Kerr, L., Ward, D., and Pate, R. (2001). Physical activity and determinants of physical activity in obese and non-obese children. *International Journal of Obesity*, 25, 822–829.

Trost, S.G., Owen, N., Bauman, A.E., Sallis, J.F., and Brown, W. (2002). Correlates of adults? Participation in physical activity: Review and update. *Medicine and Science in Sports and Exercise*, 34(12), 1996–2001.

Public Health

Vancauwenberg, J., De Bourdeaudhuij, I., Demeester, F., Van Dyke, D., Salmon, J., Clarys, P., and Deforche, B. (2011). Relationship between the physical environment and physical activity in older adults: A systematic review. *Health & Place*, 17, 458–469.

Wong, B., Faulkner, G., and Buliung, R. (2011). GIS measured environmental correlates of active school transport: A systematic review of 14 studies. *International Journal of Behavioral Nutrition and Physical Activity*, 8(39), 22.

Chapter Seven

Derivation and Validation of Metropolitan Sprawl Indices

In 1958 William Whyte in his book *The Exploding Metropolis* referred to a new notion in planning, "Suburban Sprawl," and alerted Americans that their cities were becoming more sprawling. This began the debate over sprawl and its impacts. In this and other literature, it is clear that sprawl is ordinarily conceptualized at the metropolitan level, encompassing cities and their suburbs. When we say Atlanta sprawls badly, we are probably referring to metropolitan Atlanta, not the city of Atlanta or Fulton County. The focus up to this point in the report has been on counties, because counties are typically smaller than metropolitan areas and more homogeneous than metropolitan areas. They more closely correspond to the environment in which individuals live, work, and play on a daily basis, and hence are affected by the built environment. But certain phenomena are manifested at the regional or metropolitan level, such as ozone levels and racial segregation. So in this chapter we derive metropolitan sprawl indices.

Methods

Sample

The unit of analysis in this chapter is the metropolitan area. A metropolitan area is a region that consists of a densely populated urban core and its less-populated surrounding territories that are economically and socially linked to it. The criteria for defining metropolitan areas changed in 2003. Smaller MSAs remained the same, but larger metropolitan areas, previously referred to as consolidated metropolitan statistical areas (CMSAs) are now defined as MSAs. Different portions of CMSAs, previously referred to as primary metropolitan statistical areas (PMSAs), have been redefined and reconfigured as metropolitan divisions. For example, the old New York CMSA consisted of 11 counties in two states and four PMSAs: New York PMSA, Nassau–Suffolk PMSA, Dutchess County PMSA, and Newburgh, NY-PA PMSA. The current New York MSA consists of 23 counties in three states and four metropolitan divisions. The New York MSA now is strikingly heterogeneous, whereas the old New York PMSA contained only the five boroughs that make up New York City. Metropolitan divisions do not perfectly substitute for PMSAs, as they have different size thresholds (2.5 million vs. 1 million population), but they come as close to representing homogenous units as we can come with current census geography. Metropolitan divisions are designated for each of the 11 largest MSAs.[1]

The sample in this study is limited to medium and large metropolitan areas, and metropolitan divisions where they are defined. It initially included a total of 228 areas with more than 200,000 population in 2010. The rationale for thus limiting our sample is simple: the concept of sprawl has particular relevance to large areas where the economic, social, and environmental consequences of sprawl can be significant. The concept of sprawl does not have much relevance to small MSAs such as Lewiston, ID and Casper, WY.

Parenthetically, a total of seven metropolitan areas and divisions were ultimately dropped from our sample due to the lack of Local Employment Dynamics (LED) data, a key data source for measuring sprawl. These metropolitan areas, or a portion of them, are located in Massachusetts, which does not participate in the LED program. This reduces the final sample size to 221 MSAs and metropolitan divisions.

Variables

Development Density

Low residential density is on everyone's list of sprawl indicators. Our first five density variables are the same as in the original sprawl index (Ewing et al. 2002): gross density of urban and suburban census tracts (popden), percentage of the population living at low suburban densities (lt1500), percentage of the population living at medium to high urban densities (gt12500), and urban density based on the National Land Cover Database (urbden). These variables are measured the same way for metropolitan areas as for counties (see Chapter 2).

A fifth variable is the estimated density at the center of the metropolitan area derived from a negative exponential density function (dgcent). The function assumes the form:

$$\text{Dist} = \text{Do exp } (-b \text{ dist})$$

where:

Di	=	the density of census tract i
Do	=	the estimated density at the center of the metropolitan area
b	=	the estimated density gradient or rate of decline of density with distance
dist	=	the distance of the census tract from the center of the principal city

The higher the central density, and the steeper the density function, the more compact the metropolitan area (in a monocentric sense).[2]

The sixth density variable, which is new, is analogous to the first, except it is derived with employment data from the LED database (empden). The LED data were aggregated from census block geography to generate total jobs by two-digit NAICS code for every block group in the nation. This was then divided by land area to produce a density measure.

The last two variables are related to employment centers identified by the authors as a part of this study. For more information on how the centers were identified for MSAs see "Centering" in Chapter 3. The two variables are weighted average population density (popdcen) and weighted average employment density (empdcen) of all centers within a metropolitan area. The average densities were weighted by the sum of block group jobs and residents as a percentage of the MSA total.

Land Use Mix

Segregated land uses are also on most lists of sprawl development patterns. Conversely, mixed and integrated land uses sit atop lists of pedestrian-friendly, transit-oriented, and smart growth patterns.

The first two variables in the mix factor represent the balance between jobs and population (jobpop); and the diversity of land uses (jobmix). Although using the same variables as Ewing et al. (2002) to operationalize mixed use, we computed them differently using one-mile buffers around the centers of block groups rather than computing them within the boundaries of block groups. The reason is that the latter are sensitive to the size of a block group. The larger the area, the higher the value of mixed-use variables because the block group will contain more activity in total. By using a uniform one-mile buffer, we make the unit of analysis comparable for all block groups.

The two mixed-use variables were calculated for each block group's buffer using block-level population data from the 2010 Census, and block-level employment data from the 2010 LED database. The job-population balance measure (jobpop) equals 1 for block groups with the same ratio of jobs-to-residents within the one-mile ring as the metropolitan area as a whole; 0 for block groups with only jobs or residents within the one-mile ring, not both; and intermediate values for intermediate cases. All values were weighted by the sum of block group jobs and residents as a percentage of the MSA total.[3]

The job mix variable (jobmix), an entropy measure, equals 1 for block groups with equal numbers of jobs in each sector; 0 for block groups with all jobs in a single sector within the ring; and intermediate values for intermediate cases. The sectors considered in this case were retail, entertainment, health, education, and personal services. Values were weighted by the sum of block group population and employment as a percentage of the MSA total.

A third mixed-use variable is metropolitan weighted average Walk Score (walkscore). It was computed using data from Walk Score, Inc. to measure proximity to amenities, with different amenities weighted differently and amenities discounted as the distance to them increases up to one mile and a half, where they are assumed to be no longer accessible on foot.[4] Classic Walk Score data were acquired for all urban census tracts in the U.S. Values were weighted by the sum of census tract population and employment as a percentage of the MSA total.

Activity Centering

Commercial strip development is on most lists of sprawl development patterns. The antithesis of strips is urban centers. Urban centers are concentrations of activity that provide economies of scale, facilitate modal choices and multipurpose trip making, foster an identity in the urban landscape, and are vastly different than commercial strips. This concentration, or centeredness, can relate to population or employment, and may take the form of a single dominant center or multiple subcenters. Compactness is associated with centers of all types, and sprawl with the lack of centers of any type.

Centering is the compactness dimension with the most significant improvement compared to earlier indices. Ewing et al. (2002) measured metropolitan centering in terms of concentrations of employment in or around (within three miles) historic CBDs of metropolitan areas, and at a considerable distance from (more than 10 miles) from historic CBDs. This way of measuring centering does not make much sense when applied to medium-size MSAs because most

Metropolitan Sprawl Indices

of the jobs and population fall within three miles of CBDs. It also doesn't make sense in large polycentric metropolitan areas, where historic CBDs have sometimes been eclipsed by edge cities.

The first centering variable came straight out of Ewing et al. (2002) and the 2010 Census. It is the coefficient of variation in census block group population densities, defined as the standard deviation of block group densities divided by the average density of block groups (varpop). The more variation in population densities around the mean, the more centering and/or subcentering exists within the MSA.

The second centering variable is analogous to the first, except it is derived with employment data from the LED database. It is the coefficient of variation in census block group employment densities, defined as the standard deviation of block group densities divided by the average density of block groups (varemp). The more variation in employment densities around the mean, the more centering and/or subcentering exists within the MSAs.

The third variable contributing to the centering factor is the density gradient moving outward from the CBD, estimated with a negative exponential density function. The faster density declines with distance from the center, the more centered (in a monocentric sense) the metropolitan area will be (dgrad).

The next two centering variables measure the proportion of employment and population within CBDs and employment subcenters. For computing them, we first identified the location of CBDs and employment subcenters for all metropolitan areas (see "Centering" in Chapter 3).

Out of 374 metropolitan areas in the U.S., we found 224 MSAs to be mono-centric (have only one center), 132 to be polycentric (have more than one center), and 18 metropolitan areas to have no CBD or subcenter. This procedure resulted in two new centering variables as the percentage of MSA population (popcen) and employment (empcen) in CBDs and subcenters.

Street Connectivity

Street connectivity is related to block size since smaller blocks translate into shorter and more direct routes. Large block sizes indicate a lack of street connections and alternate routes. So, three street connectivity variables were computed for each MSA based on blocks size: average block length (avgblklngh), average block size (avgblksze), and the percentage of blocks that are less than 1/100 square mile, which is the typical size of an urban block (smlblk).

These three variables were part of Ewing et al.'s original sprawl metrics. To them, we have added two new variables. They are intersection density and

Metropolitan Sprawl Indices

percentage of four-or-more way intersections. Intersections are where street connections are made and cars must stop to allow pedestrians to cross. The higher the intersection density, the more walkable the city (Jacobs 1993). Intersection density has become the most common metric in studies of built environmental impacts on individual travel behavior (Ewing and Cervero 2010).

Another common metric in such studies is the percentage of four-or-more-way intersections (Ewing and Cervero 2010). This metric provides the purest measure of street connectivity, as four-way intersections provide more routing options than three-way intersections. A high percentage of four-way intersections does not guarantee walkability, as streets may connect at four-way intersections in a super grid of arterials. But it does guarantee routing options.

For each MSA, the total number of intersections in the urbanized portion of MSA was divided by the land area to obtain intersection density (intden), while the number of four-or-more-way intersections was multiplied by 100 and divided by the total number of intersections to obtain the percentage of four-or-more way intersections (4–way).

Individual Compactness/Sprawl Factors

For each dimension of sprawl, we ran principal component analysis on the measured variables, and the principal component that captured the largest share of common variance among the measured variables was selected to represent that dimension. Factor loadings (the correlation between a variable and a principal component), eigenvalues (the explanatory power of a single principal component), and percentages of explained variance are shown in Table 7.1.

The eigenvalue of the density factor is 5.82, which indicates that this one factor accounts for about three quarters of the total variance in the dataset. As anticipated, the percentage of the population living at less than 1,500 persons per square mile loads negatively on the density factor. The rest load positively. The eigenvalue for the mix factor is 2.30, which indicates that this one factor accounts for more than three quarters of the total variance in the dataset. All component variables load positively on the mix factor. The eigenvalue of the centering factor is 1.90, which indicates that this factor accounts for about 38 percent of the total variance in the datasets. The density gradient loads negatively on centering factor as expected. The rest load positively. The eigenvalue of the street factor is 2.51, which indicates that this factor accounts for more than a half of the total variance in the dataset. As expected, the average block size and average block length load negatively on the street connectivity factor. The rest load positively.

Table 7.1: Variable Loadings of Four Factors for 2010

Component Matrix		Data Sources	Factor Loadings
Density factor			
popden	gross population density	Census 2010	0.900
empden	gross employment density	LED 2010	0.898
lt1500	percentage of the population living at low suburban densities	Census 2010	−0.597
gt12500	percentage of the population living at medium to high urban densities	Census 2010	0.879
urbden	net population density of urban lands	NLCD	0.925
dgcent	estimated density at the center of the metro area derived from a negative exponential density function	Census 2010, Tiger 2010	0.948
popdcen	weighted average population density of centers	Census 2010	0.810
empdcen	weighted average employment density of centers	LED 2010	0.817
Eigenvalue			5.82
Explained variance			72.80%
Mix use factor			
jobpop	job-population balance	LED 2010	0.834
jobmix	degree of job mixing (entropy)	LED 2010	0.921
walkscore	weighted average Walk Score	Walk Score Inc.	0.870
Eigenvalue			2.30
Explained variance			76.72%
Centering factor			
varpop	coefficient of variation in census block group population densities	Census 2010	0.495
varemp	coefficient of variation in census block group employment densities	LED 2010	0.313
dgrad	density gradient moving outward from the CBD	Census 2010, Tiger 2010	−0.375
popcen	percentage of MSA population in CBD or sub-centers	Census 2010	0.833
empcen	percentage of MSA employment in CBD or sub-centers	LED 2010	0.847
Eigenvalue			1.90
Explained variance			37.89%

Metropolitan Sprawl Indices

Table 7.1: Continued

Component Matrix		Data Sources	Factor Loadings
Street factor			
smlblk	percentage of small urban blocks	Census 2010	0.871
avgblksze	average block size	Census 2010	−0.804
avgblklng	average block length	NAVTEQ 2012	−0.649
intden	intersection density	TomTom 2007	0.729
4way	percentage of 4-or-more-way intersections	TomTom 2007	0.380
Eigenvalue			2.51
Explained variance			50.03%

Overall Compactness/Sprawl Index for 2010

Although density has received more attention as a dimension of sprawl than have other factors, similar to Ewing et al. (2002) we could think of no rationale for giving different weights to the four factors. All four factors affect the accessibility or inaccessibility of development patterns. Each factor can move a MSA along the continuum from sprawl to compact development. Thus the four were simply summed, in effect giving each dimension of sprawl equal weight in the overall index.

The second and more difficult issue was whether to, and how to, adjust the resulting sprawl index for MSA size. As areas grow, so do their labor and real estate markets, and their land prices. Their density gradients accordingly shift upward, and other measures of compactness (intersection density, for example) follow suit. The simple correlation between the sum of the four sprawl factors and the population of the MSA is 0.575, significant at .001 probability level. Thus, the largest urbanized areas, perceived as the most sprawling by the public, actually appear less sprawling than smaller urbanized areas when sprawl is measured strictly in terms of the four factors, with no consideration given to area size.

We used the same methodology as Ewing et al. (2002) to account for metropolitan area size. We regressed the sum of the four sprawl factors on the natural logarithm of the population of the MSAs. The standardized residuals became the overall measure of sprawl. As such, this index is uncorrelated with the log of population. In effect, with this transformation, the degree of sprawl for each metropolitan area is being measured relative to other metropolitan areas of comparable size. However, the overall index still has a high correlation (r=0.866) with the sum of four factors before adjustment.

We transformed the overall sprawl index into a metric with a mean of 100 and a standard deviation of 25 for ease of use and understanding. More compact metropolitans have index values above 100, while the more sprawling have values below 100. Table 7.2 presents overall compactness scores and individual component scores for the 10 most compact and the 10 most sprawling large metropolitan areas. By these metrics, New York and San Francisco are the most compact large metropolitan divisions (see Figure 7.1), while Hickory, NC and Atlanta, GA are the most sprawling metropolitan areas (see Figure 7.2). These figures are at the same scale, and it is clear that the urban footprints of the former are more concentrated than those of the latter. Again all metropolitan areas and divisions in Massachusetts, including the Boston metropolitan division, are not in the list due to the lack of available employment data (LED) for this state.

Relationship to Transportation Outcomes

We used data from the 2011 American Community Survey (ACS), five-year estimates to validate our sprawl metrics. First, we computed average vehicle ownership per household, walk and transit mode shares, and average drive times for census metropolitan areas and divisions. Then, from the 2010 Census, we downloaded data on gender, age, race, household size, and computed percentages and mean values to describe socioeconomic status. These are control variables. We acquired gasoline price data at the MSA level from the Oil Price Information Service. Retail prices are average prices from samples of stations in each MSA and are reported with all relevant taxes included. These prices are the true-posted "sign" prices (as they would appear outside a gas station). Average gasoline price is another control variable. Table 7.3 shows a list of all dependent and independent variables used in the validation.

We estimated two sets of regression models. Our first set of regressions used the overall compactness index for 2010 (index) as an independent variable. The second set of regressions used the four compactness/sprawl factors individually (denfac, mixfac, cenfac, and strfac) as independent variables. In both sets of regressions, the dependent variables were logged so as to be normally distributed and all independent variables were also transformed into log form to achieve a better fit with the data, reduce the influence of outliers, and adjust for nonlinearity of the data. The transformations had the added advantage of allowing us to interpret regression coefficients as elasticities.

Results for models with the overall compactness index are presented in Table 7.4. Control variables mostly have the expected signs and often are significant. The compactness index (index) has the expected strong positive relationships

Table 7.2: Compactness/Sprawl Scores for 10 Most Compact and 10 Most Sprawling Metropolitan Areas and Divisions in 2010

Rank		Index	denfac	mixfac	cenfac	strfac
10 most compact metropolitan areas						
1	New York-White Plains-Wayne, NY-NJ Metro Division	203.4	384.3	159.3	213.5	193.8
2	San Francisco-San Mateo-Redwood City, CA Metro Division	194.3	185.9	167.2	230.9	162.8
3	Atlantic City-Hammonton, NJ Metro Area	150.4	96.3	100.1	154.5	130.7
4	Santa Barbara-Santa Maria-Goleta, CA Metro Area	146.6	112.3	148.9	109.5	122.1
5	Champaign-Urbana, IL Metro Area	145.2	100.0	123.3	153.6	82.8
6	Santa Cruz-Watsonville, CA Metro Area	145.0	98.9	146.2	107.9	112.2
7	Trenton-Ewing, NJ Metro Area	144.7	115.9	128.0	97.4	139.1
8	Miami-Miami Beach-Kendall, FL Metro Division	144.1	160.2	136.4	117.9	166.9
9	Springfield, IL Metro Area	142.2	90.4	100.5	160.0	96.7
10	Santa Ana-Anaheim-Irvine, CA Metro Division	139.9	161.19	155.0	79.6	181.8
10 most sprawling metropolitan areas						
212	Kingsport-Bristol-Bristol, TN-VA Metro Area	60.0	78.7	40.5	89.7	82.9
213	Augusta-Richmond County, GA-SC Metro Area	59.2	85.2	60.7	88.5	73.9
214	Greenville-Mauldin-Easley, SC Metro Area	59.0	86.7	72.9	81.1	71.4
215	Riverside-San Bernardino-Ontario, CA Metro Area	56.2	103.7	111.2	77.0	80.3
216	Baton Rouge, LA Metro Area	55.6	91.3	72.0	69.7	80.4
217	Nashville-Davidson—Murfreesboro—Franklin, TN Metro Area	51.7	91.5	63.9	96.2	77.0
218	Prescott, AZ Metro Area	49.0	82.3	53.2	58.2	70.0
219	Clarksville, TN-KY Metro Area	41.5	84.5	39.7	74.5	60.8
220	Atlanta-Sandy Springs-Marietta, GA Metro Area	41.0	97.8	85.5	89.9	75.9
221	Hickory-Lenoir-Morganton, NC Metro Area	24.9	78.6	40.5	67.0	56.9

Figure 7.1: Most Compact Metropolitan Areas (New York and San Francisco)

Figure 7.2: Most Sprawling Metropolitan Areas (Atlanta and Hickory, NC)

Metropolitan Sprawl Indices

Table 7.3: Variables Used to Explain Transportation Outcomes (all variables log transformed)

Variables		Data sources
Dependent variables		
walkshr	percentage of commuters walking to work	ACS 2007–2011
transitshr	percentage of commuters using public transportation	ACS 2007–2011
hhveh	average vehicle ownership per household	ACS 2007–2011
drivetime	average journey-to-work drive time in minutes	ACS 2007–2011
Independent variables		
pop	metropolitan population	Census 2010
hhsize	average household size	Census 2010
age1524	percentage of population 15-24 years old	Census 2010
male	percentage of male population	Census 2010
white	percentage of white population	Census 2010
income	income per capita	ACS 2007–2011
fuel	average fuel price for the metropolitan area	OPIS database 2010
index	MSA compactness index for 2010	computed
denfac	density factor (a weighted combination of 8 density variables)	computed
mixfac	mix factor (a weighted combination of 3 mixed-use variables)	computed
cenfac	centering factor (a weighted combination of 5 centering variables)	computed
strfac	street factor (a weighted combination of 5 street-related variables)	computed

to walk and transit mode shares, and the expected negative relationship to average drive time and average vehicle ownership per household. As noted, the coefficients of these log–log models are elasticities. For every percentage increase in the compactness index, the walk mode share increases by 0.39 percent, the transit mode share increases by 1.15 percent, the average drive time declines by 0.05 percent, and average vehicle ownership declines by 0.06 percent. Based on these results, we consider the overall compactness index to be validated.

The new multidimensional compactness factors are mostly significant with the expected signs (see Table 7.5). The density factor, denfac, and centering factor, cenfac, are the most important correlates of walking, followed by the mix factor, mixfac. The density factor is also the most important correlate of transit

Metropolitan Sprawl Indices

Table 7.4: Relationships of the Overall Compactness Index to Transportation Outcomes (log-log transformed – t-statistics in parentheses)

	walkshr	transitshr	drivetime	hhveh
constant	−11.86	−0.62	4.69	−6.01
pop	0.01(0.44)	0.42(8.35)***	0.04(3.79)***	−0.01(−1.28)
hhsize	−0.65(−1.92)*	0.69(1.24)	0.40(3.81)***	0.80(9.07)***
age1524	1.47(9.19)***	1.74(6.61)***	−0.15(−3.40)***	0.13(3.02)**
male	−0.79(-0.45)	−10.63(−3.66)***	−0.99(−1.90)	0.82(1.79)
white	0.55(3.65)***	0.21(0.83)	−0.15(−3.27)***	0.12(3.03)**
income	0.55(3.33)***	2.14(7.80)***	0.25(4.51)***	0.25(5.80)***
fuel	2.45(5.18)***	3.35(4.28)***	0.21(1.49)	−0.88(−7.17)***
index	0.39(4.22)***	1.15(7.57)***	−0.05(−1.85)	−0.06(-2.45)**
adjusted R2	0.54	0.73	0.48	0.42

* .05 probability level
** .01 probability level
*** .001 probability level

use, followed by the centering factor, mix factor, and street factor. All of compactness factors but street connectivity have negative signs in the drive time equation. Mix and street factors are the most significant, followed by the density factor. Street factor is positively related to average drive time. This may be due to the increased wait time at intersections in a dense street network. All of the compactness factors are inversely related to vehicle ownership per household, although only three, the density factor, mix factor, and street factor, are statistically significant.

Theoretically, we do not expect four factors to be equally important for all travel outcomes. For example, a concentration of activities is necessary to support investment and use of transit. So as one would expect, the centering factor is the most significant correlate of transit mode share and has the second highest elasticity.

Discussion

This chapter uses the same basic methodology as Ewing et al. (2002) to measure the extent of sprawl for medium and large metropolitan areas and divisions in 2010. However, we have expanded the sample size from 83 metropolitan areas in Ewing et al. (2002) to the 221 MSAs in this study. And, of course, metropolitan boundaries have changed between the censuses.

Metropolitan Sprawl Indices

Table 7.5: Relationships of Individual Compactness Factors to Transportation Outcomes (log-log transformed – t-statistics in parentheses)

	walkshr	transitshr	drivetime	hhveh
constant	−11.84	−1.73	2.62	−4.04
pop	−0.09(−2.51)**	0.18(3.09)***	0.06(5.69)***	0.03(3.08)**
hhsize	−0.54(−1.63)	0.86(1.50)	0.54(5.41)***	0.77(9.57)***
age1524	1.25(7.99)***	1.60(5.91)***	−0.07(−1.56)	0.11(2.89)**
male	−0.96(−0.58)	−10.85(−3.82)***	0.62(−1.30)	0.63(1.59)
white	0.63(4.28)***	0.30(1.20)	−0.13(−3.05)**	0.04(1.10)
income	0.44(2.77)**	2.05(7.49)***	0.32(6.22)***	0.24(6.23)***
fuel	1.92(4.15)***	3.05(3.80)***	0.44(3.31)**	−0.91(−8.11)***
denfac	0.82(3.69)***	0.83(2.14)*	−0.32(−2.79)**	−0.37(−6.94)***
mixfac	0.25(2.13)**	0.60(2.89)**	−0.14(−3.84)***	−0.14(−4.79)***
cenfac	0.36(3.81)***	0.73(4.41)***	−0.01(−0.25)	−0.01(−0.52)
strfac	−0.23(−1.93)	0.37(1.81)	0.16(4.58)***	−0.06(−2.24) *
adjusted R2	0.605	0.743	0.578	0.564

* .05 probability level
** .01 probability level
*** .001 probability level

For the 76 areas that are included in both studies, the compactness rankings are generally consistent across years. The Spearman correlation between the compactness rankings in 2000 and 2010 is 0.635, significant at .001 probability level, which indicates that, in general, compact areas in 2000 are still compact in 2010; and the sprawling areas in 2000 are still sprawling. New York is the most compact region followed by San Francisco in both years. Atlanta is the fourth most sprawling area in 2000 and the second most sprawling area in 2010. Riverside–San Bernardino–Ontario, CA is the most sprawling in 2000 and the seventh most sprawling area in 2010.

There are, however, metropolitan areas with significantly different ranking in 2010 than 2000. In a fast-growing area, a lot of development can occur in 10 years. One of the surprising cases is the Las Vegas–Paradise, NV metropolitan area. Its ranking rose from the 30th most compact area in 2000 to the 16th in 2010 due to its moderate to high score in all four dimensions. This is consistent with the Fulton et al. (2001) study that found Las Vegas is getting more compact. "Las Vegas led the nation with an increase in its metropolitan density of 50 percent, thus rising in the overall density rankings from 114th in 1982 to 14th in 1997" (Fulton et al. 2001).

Metropolitan Sprawl Indices

Refinements in operationalizing sprawl are another reason for differences in rankings between years. Land-use mix and activity centering are the two dimensions with the most significant changes. As contributors to centering, we now consider not only CBDs but employment subcenters. The existence of subcenters is what distinguishes polycentric regions from monocentric regions. The Washington DC metropolitan division is an example of polycentric region. As shown in Figure 7.3, we identified 11 subcenters (light gray color) in the metropolitan division. Out of 76 metropolitan areas with rankings in both years, the Washington DC metropolitan division has the 27th highest score for activity centering in 2010 while it had the 41st highest score in 2000. Its overall compactness ranking rose from 52nd most compact in 2000 to 27th most compact in 2010 due to its change in the centering score.

We also standardized the unit of analysis for mix-use metrics by measuring them with one-mile buffers around the centroid of block groups. Out of 76 areas that are included in both years, Phoenix has the 19th highest mix factor

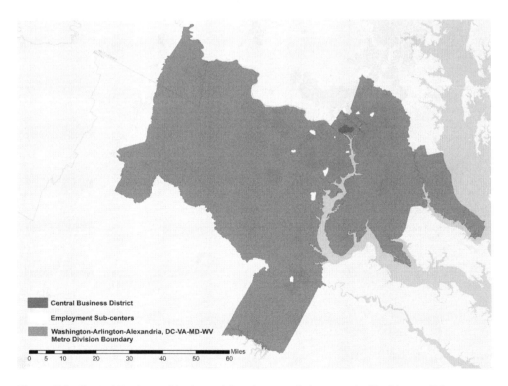

Figure 7.3: Central Business District and Employment Subcenters in Washington DC Metropolitan Division

Metropolitan Sprawl Indices

score in 2000 while it has the 24th lowest mix score in 2010. As a result, the Phoenix metropolitan area's overall ranking drops from 18th most compact in 2000 to 14th most sprawling in 2010.

Finally, the changes in compactness score in some areas are due to changes in metropolitan boundaries. Out of 76 metropolitan areas in both samples, Detroit moved up from 14th most sprawling in 2000 to 12th most compact in 2010. The 2010 Detroit, MI metropolitan division covers only about a fifth of the area of the 2000 Detroit PMSA. The division is mostly limited to the Detroit's downtown and surroundings. The lowest-density portions of Detroit PMSA are not included in 2010 metropolitan division (see Figure 7.4). In particular, Warren-Troy-Farmington Hills, MI is now its own metropolitan division, and a very sprawling one, the 21th most sprawling out of 221 metropolitan areas in 2010.

In 1997, the *Journal of the American Planning Association* published a pair of point-counterpoint articles now listed by the American Planning Association

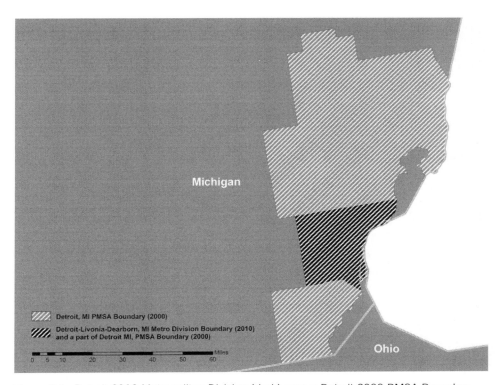

Figure 7.4: Detroit 2010 Metropolitan Division (dark) versus Detroit 2000 PMSA Boundary (light)

Metropolitan Sprawl Indices

as "classics" in the urban planning literature. In the first article, "Are Compact Cities Desirable?" Peter Gordon and Harry Richardson argued in favor of urban sprawl as a benign response to consumer preferences. In the counterpoint article, "Is Los Angeles-Style Sprawl Desirable?" Reid Ewing argued for compact cities as an alternative to sprawl. They disagreed at the time about almost everything: the characteristics, causes, and costs of sprawl, and the cures for any costs associated with sprawl.

In their original debate, Ewing challenged the notion that Los Angeles is compact, while Gordon and Richardson labeled planning initiatives in Portland ineffective. The Los Angeles metropolitan division, with a new compactness index of 136.7, ranks as the 21st most compact metropolitan area in the U.S. among 221 MSAs in our sample. In a parallel analysis focusing on urbanized areas (see Chapter 9), Los Angeles saw an impressive rise in its compactness ranking, from 18th in 2000 to 8th in 2010. The reason: infill development.

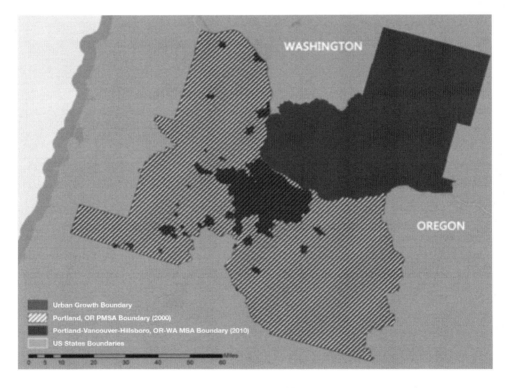

Figure 7.5: Portland Metropolitan Area Boundary in 2010 versus Portland PMSA Boundary in 2000

Metropolitan Sprawl Indices

"Contradicting metropolitan L.A.'s reputation as the capital of unbridled sprawl, roughly two-thirds of new housing built there between 2005 and 2009 was infill – constructed in previously developed areas rather than on raw land in the exurbs" (Boxall 2012). Los Angeles is certainly more compact today than suggested by Ewing in 1997.

The change in Portland's compactness ranking is also interesting. Portland fell from the sixth most compact in 2000 to 80th in 2010 because of boundary changes. The high ranking in 2000 applied to the Portland PMSA, basically the area subject to an urban growth boundary. The metropolitan area now includes Vancouver, WA, and its surroundings, in addition to the Portland PMSA (as shown in Figure 7.5). The new area is all outside the urban growth boundary (UGB).

Notes

1　The metropolitan divisions, as components of MSAs, somewhat resemble PMSAs under the old system. However, PMSAs were much more common. The higher population threshold for establishing metropolitan divisions (at least 2.5 million), opposed to the threshold of at least 1 million to establish PMSAs, means that the new system contains 29 metropolitan divisions within 11 MSAs, compared to 73 PMSAs within 18 CMSAs under the old system.

2　The function was estimated as follows. The principal cities of the metro areas were identified as the first-named cities in the 1990 definitions of those areas. Their centers were determined by locating CBD tracts within the principal cities as specified in the 1980 STF3 file. 1980 designations were adopted because CBDs have not been designated since then. The means of the latitudes and longitudes of the centroids of those CBD tracts were taken as the metropolitan centers. The distances from the centers to all tracts were calculated using an ArcGIS. Finally, a negative exponential density function was fit to the resulting data points to estimate the intercept and density gradient.

3　See "land-use mix" section for the formula used for computing job–population balance and job-mix measures.

4　A grocery store, for example, gets three times the weight of a book store. The distance decay function starts with a value of 100 and decays to 75 percent at a half mile, 12.5 percent at one mile, and zero at 1.5 miles.

References

Boxall, B. (2012). Infill Housing Development Rises in Los Angeles Region. *Los Angeles Times*, 20 December. Available online at: http://articles.latimes.com/2012/dec/20/science/la-sci-sn-infill-housing-increases20121220 (last accessed 5 May 2017).

Ewing, R. (1997). Is Los Angeles-style sprawl desirable? *Journal of the American Planning Association*, 63(1), 107–126.

Ewing, R., and Cervero, R. (2010). Travel and the built environment: A meta-analysis. *Journal of the American Planning Association*, 76(3), 265–294.

Ewing, R., Pendall, R., and Chen, D. (2002). *Measuring Sprawl and Its Impacts*. Smart Growth America, Washington, D.C.

Fulton, W., Pendall, R., Nguyen,. M., and Harrison, A. (2001). *Who Sprawls Most? How Growth Patterns Differ Across the U.S.*, Center for Urban & Metropolitan Policy, The Brookings Institution, Washington, D.C.

Gordon, P., and Richardson, H.W. (1997). Are compact cities a desirable planning goal? *Journal of the American Planning Association*, 63(1), 95–106.

Jacobs, A.B. (1993). *Great Streets*. MIT Press, Cambridge, MA.

Whyte, W.H. (1958). *The Exploding Metropolis.* Doubleday, Garden City, N.Y.

Chapter Eight

Relationship of Sprawl to Topical Outcomes

Urban planners are ultimately less interested in development patterns, per se, than in the costs and benefits of one pattern versus another. That is to say, there are no inherently good or bad patterns, only good or bad outcomes. The loaded term "sprawl" has come to be applied to certain development patterns because of their documented negative outcomes.

The literature on impacts of sprawl is well established. Researchers have studied impacts of sprawl on quality-of-life outcomes such as housing affordability (Kahn 2001; 2006; Wassmer and Baass 2006); traffic congestion (Ewing et al. 2002; Zolnik 2011; Holcombe and Williams 2012); traffic safety (Ewing et al. 2003b; Trowbridge et al. 2009); physical activity and obesity (Ewing et al. 2003a; Kelly-Schwartz et al. 2004; Sturm and Cohen 2004; Doyle et al. 2006; Plantinga and Bernell 2007; Fan and Song 2009; Lee et al. 2009); social capital (Kim et al. 2006; Nguyen 2010); and air quality (Kahn 2006; Stone 2008; Schweitzer and Zhou 2010; Stone et al. 2010; Bereitschaft and Debbage 2013).

There are, however, other potential outcomes of sprawl that have made the news recently. There is little understanding on how urban sprawl may affect so-called "topical outcomes" such as life expectancy, upward mobility, and housing costs. In this chapter we seek to find out how urban sprawl may affect these outcomes.

Life Expectancy

The literature points to several important sociodemographic variables that affect life expectancy, including gender (women live longer than men), income (higher income people live longer), race (whites live longer than nonwhites), and education (in part due to an income effect, those with more education live longer).

Mirowsky and Ross (2000) hypothesized that American adults can expect longer lives the higher their achieved socioeconomic status. Three aspects of socioeconomic status provide an outline for analysis: education, employment and occupation, and economic well-being. Each has known or suspected effects on health and survival that may shape subjective estimates of life expectancy.

Ezzati et al. (2008) analyzed the trends in county mortality and cross-county mortality disparities, including the contributions of specific diseases to county-level mortality trends. There are large disparities in health and mortality across population subgroups defined by race, income, geography, social class, education, and community deprivation indices.

Education regulates access to occupations, and affects both personal earnings and household income. Persons with less than a high school diploma have twice the age-adjusted mortality rate as those with college degrees (Rogers 1992; Christenson and Johnson 1995; Elo and Preston 1996). Education also improves physical health and functioning net of employment status, occupational status, job quality, earnings, household income, race, sex, age, and social origins (Johnson and Wolinsky 1993; Ross and Wu 1995; Reynolds and Ross 1998).

Olshansky et al. (2005) analyzed the substantial rise in the prevalence of obesity and its life-shortening implications. The study found that there are also other threats to life expectancy. Forces such as infectious diseases, pollution, lack of regular exercise, ineffective blood-pressure screening, tobacco use, and stress can lead to a reduction in life expectancy.

Shaw et al. (2005) studied the determinants of life expectancy in developed countries. They argued that life expectancy is predetermined by behavioral and policy variables in what can be loosely described as a production function for health. While empirical results are mixed, the general consensus is that population life expectancy is a function of environmental measures (e.g., wealth, education, safety regulations, infrastructure), lifestyle measures (e.g., fruit and vegetable consumption; tobacco or alcohol consumption), and health care consumption measures (e.g., medical or pharmaceutical expenditures).

Conceptual Framework

There are at least four plausible causal pathways between sprawl and life expectancy—one through obesity, which Chapter 6 determined to be higher in sprawling counties due, most likely, to reduced levels of physical activity. Obesity is the second leading preventable cause of death in the U.S. (Mokdad et al. 2004).

Relationship of Sprawl to Topical Outcomes

A second pathway is through traffic fatalities, which Chapter 5 found to be higher in sprawling counties due to increased driving and crash exposure. There are upwards of 32,000 traffic fatalities in the U.S. each year, many involving young people who die prematurely. Traffic fatalities are the leading cause of death for those aged 15 through 24 (Kochanek et al., 2011). Traffic fatalities are the sixth leading preventable cause of death in the U.S. (Mokdad et al. 2004).

A third pathway is through air pollution. Four studies have related sprawl to poor air quality (Ewing 2002; Stone 2008; Schweitzer and Zhou, 2010; Bereitschaft and Debbage 2013). The most recent and most comprehensive found that metropolitan areas with lower levels of sprawl on average exhibit lower concentrations of ozone (O3) and fine particulates (PM2.5) (Bereitschaft and Debbage 2013). Countless studies have related air quality to illness and premature death.

A fourth pathway is through violent crime, or specifically, homicide. Central cities are generally considered more crime ridden than suburbs and exurbs. However, we know of no study that has explicitly related compactness or sprawl to violent crime. One study did compare the mortality risk associated with leaving home across 15 metropolitan areas, and found that when traffic fatalities and homicides-by-strangers were summed, central cities and inner suburbs were actually safer than outer areas (Lucy 2003). Another study reached a similar conclusion when it compared injury deaths (traffic, homicide, suicide, etc.) across an urban–rural continuum, and found major cities to be safer than rural areas (Myers et al. 2013).

The literatures on sprawl and traffic safety, and sprawl and obesity, have already been reviewed in Chapters 5 and 6. Here we summarily review the literatures on the other two causal pathways.

Air Pollution

Ozone and particulates are the most widespread air pollutants. Ground level ozone is not emitted directly into the air, but is created by chemical reactions between nitrogen oxides (NOx) and volatile organic compounds (VOCs) in the presence of sunlight. Emissions from industrial facilities and electric utilities, motor vehicle exhaust, gasoline vapors, and chemical solvents are some of the major sources of NOx and VOCs. The sources of PM2.5 include emissions from automobiles, power plants, wood burning, industrial processes, and diesel-powered vehicles. These fine particles are also formed in the atmosphere when gases such as sulfur dioxide, NOx, and VOCs (all of which are also products of fuel combustion) are transformed in the air by chemical reactions. Since motor vehicles are a major source of both ozone precursors and PM2.5 components and precursors, it is not unreasonable to expect some relationship between sprawl and both ozone and PM2.5 concentrations, and hence between sprawl and life expectancy.

Nearly 132 million people live in counties where monitors show unhealthy levels of one or both. Ozone can harm lung function, irritate the respiratory system, and cause asthma, bronchitis, other cardiopulmonary problems, and premature death (Levy et al. 2001; World Health Organization 2003). Particle pollution can increase the risk of heart disease, lung cancer, asthma attacks, and premature death (Dockery 2009). A recent study estimates that ozone and PM2.5 cause about the same number of deaths each year in North America (Silva et al. 2013). The estimated numbers are between 34,400 and 52,200 for ozone, and between 43,000 and 77,000 for PM2.5.

An Air Quality Index (AQI) has been estimated at the county level by EPA and includes an annual summary of days with good, moderate, unhealthy, and very unhealthy air. The AQI takes into account all six criteria air pollutants: carbon monoxide, nitrogen dioxide, ozone, sulfur dioxide, PM2.5, and PM10. Each row of the AQI Report lists summary values for one year and one county. The summary values include both quantitative measures (days of the year having "unhealthy" air quality, for example) and descriptive statistics (median AQI values, for example).

Crime

It may be thought that larger, denser cities are more plagued by crime than smaller cities and towns, but research has shown that this is not always the case. According to Browning et al. (2010), there may be higher crime rates when density begins to increase initially, but once it reaches a certain level and there is more pedestrian activity and traffic due to higher density, crime rates will likely decrease. However, this decrease in crime at higher densities could also be due to increased policing that tends to come along with mixed-use development, among other factors such as community cohesion, availability of economic opportunities, and higher education and income levels of residents in larger cities (Browning et al. 2010; Litman 2013).

A Brookings Institution Study analyzed data from the Uniform Crime Report (UCR) and the American Community Survey (ACS) and found that the violent crime rate in cities dropped by 29 percent compared to the violent crime rate in suburbs, which dropped only 7 percent (Kneebone and Raphael 2011). Although the overall rate of crime is still higher in cities than in suburbs, the difference between the two is narrowing.

Relationship of Sprawl to Topical Outcomes

While crime may be higher in cities, this doesn't mean that cities are less safe overall. Myers et al. (2013) analyzed injury death rates in both urban and rural environments, and found that, overall, the occurrence of serious injuries resulting in death was 20 percent higher in rural areas than urban areas. The researchers state that the risk of homicide is indeed higher in urban areas, but this is outweighed by deaths resulting from motor vehicle crashes, among other injuries, in rural areas (Myers et al. 2013). In fact, the risk of fatality due to motor vehicle crash is two times higher in rural than urban areas (Myers et al. 2013). Similarly, another study looked at the dangers of leaving one's home in terms of rate of homicide by strangers and motor vehicle or traffic fatalities and compared these risks in rural and urban areas (Lucy 2003). The results again showed higher rates of traffic fatalities and homicides by strangers in rural areas with lower population densities (Lucy 2003).

When looking at violent crime, its effect on life expectancy varies. Redelings et al. (2010) found that homicide reduced life expectancy by 0.4 years for residents in Los Angeles County, but it reduced life expectancy for black males by 2.1 years, a stark difference. The Centers for Disease Control (CDC) finds that discrepancies in life expectancy exist between difference races. The CDC reports that life expectancy for the black population was 3.8 years lower than the white population (4.7 years lower for black males compared to white males) due to factors such as health issues and homicide rates (Kochanek et al. 2013). Crime may play a role in life expectancy, but it is dependent on the economic and social characteristics of a particular city or neighborhood.

Methods

In this section we use a recently released dataset of life expectancies by county (Wang et al. 2013) to study the relationship between sprawl and life expectancy. The release of this dataset made the national news, as the media realized that where you live could affect the length as well as the quality of your life.[1]

Differences across counties were surprisingly large. The mean life expectancy for males and females combined was just over 78 years. The standard deviation was more than two years. The range was 71 years at the bottom to 83 years at the top.

The dataset came with no explanation as to differences in life span from place to place. In this section, we use structural equation modeling (SEM) to estimate a model of life expectancy. Readers are referred to Chapter 5 for a description of SEM and its advantages in cases like this with complex interrelationships among variables.

Relationship of Sprawl to Topical Outcomes

The variables tested in the model are shown in Table 8.1. The variable of greatest interest is lifeexp, county average life expectancy. There are four mediating (intermediate) variables: average county-level crash rates per 100,000 population (crash), EPA's AQI90 (a combination of six air quality indicators), average county BMI, and the violent crime rate (crime). They relate, respectively, to four causes of premature death: traffic accidents, respiratory illnesses, obesity-related chronic health conditions, and crime and its effects on physical and mental health.

Results

We have estimated an SE model for life expectancy with Amos 19.0, a popular SEM software package with a good graphic display. The fitted model is shown in Figure 8.1. The path diagram is copied directly from Amos. Causal pathways are represented by straight uni-directional arrows. Correlations are represented by curved bi-directional arrows (the already complex causal diagram, some correlations are omitted). By convention, circles represent error terms in the model, of which there is one for each endogenous (response) variable.

Table 8.1: County Variables (variables log transformed)

Variables		Data Sources
Endogenous Variables		
lifeexp	average life expectancy	States, Census 2010
crash	annual crashes per 100,000 population	State transportation agencies
AQI90	90th percentile air quality index	EPA
BMI	average body mass index	BRFSS
crime	violent crime rate per 100,000 population	FBI Uniform Crime Statistics
Exogenous Variables		
pop	metropolitan population	Census 2010
SES	Yost's Socioeconomic Status metric	National Institutes of Health
white	percentage of white population	Census 2010
index	county compactness index for 2010 (including additional variables compared to 2000 index)	

Relationship of Sprawl to Topical Outcomes

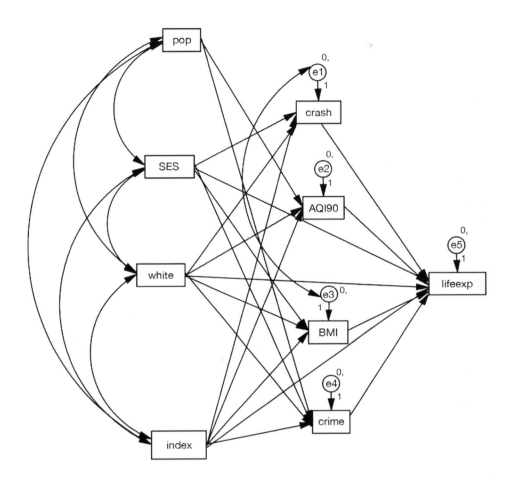

Figure 8.1: Causal Path Diagram for Life Expectancy in Terms of County Compactness and Other Variables

Direct relationships are presented in Table 8.2. Maximum likelihood methods were used in the estimations. Model evaluation was based on four factors: (1) theoretical soundness; (2) chi-square tests of absolute model fit; (3) root-mean-square errors of approximation (RMSEA), which unlike the chi-square, correct for sample size; and (4) comparative fit indices (CFI).

Relationships are highly significant and generally as expected. Goodness-of-fit measures at the bottom of the table suggest that the model provides a good fit to the data (see Chapter 5 for a discussion of these measures). The life expectancy model in Figure 8.1 has a chi-square of 8.3 with 9 model degrees

Relationship of Sprawl to Topical Outcomes

of freedom and a p-value of 0.503. The low chi-square relative to model degrees of freedom and a high (>0.05) p-value are indicators of good model fit.

The county compactness index has a direct positive relationship to life expectancy, plus indirect effects through mediating variables. Compactness affects mortality directly, but the causal mechanism is unclear. It may be, for example, that sprawling areas have higher traffic speeds and longer emergency response times, lower quality and less accessible health care facilities, or less availability of healthy foods.

Table 8.2: Direct Effects of Variables on One Another in the Life Expectancy Model

			coefficient	std error	critical ratio	p-value
crash	<—	index	−0.02	0.113	−0.178	0.859
AQI90	<—	index	1.778	4.302	0.413	0.679
BMI	<—	index	−0.046	0.015	−3.094	0.002
crime	<—	index	1.156	0.137	8.439	<0.001
BMI	<—	SES	−0.063	0.01	−6.121	<0.001
BMI	<—	white	−0.02	0.012	−1.697	0.09
AQI90	<—	pop	2.681	0.534	5.018	<0.001
crash	<—	white	−0.198	0.09	−2.201	0.028
crash	<—	SES	−0.281	0.079	−3.575	<0.001
crime	<—	white	−1.365	0.115	−11.838	<0.001
crime	<—	SES	−0.665	0.11	−6.035	<0.001
crime	<—	pop	−0.049	0.02	−2.49	0.013
AQI90	<—	white	−9.149	3.429	−2.668	0.008
lifeexp	<—	BMI	−0.036	0.012	−3.082	0.002
lifeexp	<—	AQI90	0	0	−0.327	0.744
lifeexp	<—	crash	−0.01	0.002	−6.397	<0.001
lifeexp	<—	SES	0.057	0.003	17.491	<0.001
lifeexp	<—	index	0.04	0.005	8.833	<0.001
lifeexp	<—	crime	−0.008	0.001	−6.049	<0.001
lifeexp	<—	white	0.009	0.004	2.322	0.02
chi-square			8.3			
			degrees of freedom = 9			
			p-value = 0.503			
RMSEA			0.0			
			p-value = 0.989			
CFI			1.0			

Let's consider each indirect effect in turn. The compactness index is negatively but weakly related to crash rates, which in turn are negatively related to life expectancy. This is as expected from Chapter 5, given the mixed relationships between compactness and traffic safety. Hence the indirect effect of compactness on life expectancy via this causal pathway is de minimis. The compactness index is also negatively related to BMI, which is negatively related to life expectancy. This is as expected from Chapter 6. Hence the indirect effect of compactness on life expectancy via this causal pathway is positive The compactness index is positively but weakly related to the AQI, which in this analysis appears unrelated to life expectancy. This causal pathway is also de minimis. Finally, the compactness index is positively related to violent crime, which is negatively related to life expectancy. Hence the indirect effect of compactness on life expectancy via this causal pathway is negative. This squares with popular notions that, in terms of crime, urban areas are more dangerous than suburban areas.

Direct, indirect, and total effects of variables on one another are shown in Table 8.3. The net indirect effect of compactness on life expectancy is negative, but this effect is overwhelmed by the direct positive effect of compactness on life expectancy. Using life expectancy data from a credible source, and our validated compactness/sprawl index, we conclude that life expectancy is significantly higher in compact than sprawling counties. As the compactness index doubles (increases by 100 percent), life expectancy increases by about 3.3 percent. For the average American with a life expectancy of 78 years, this translates into a two and a half year difference. That is well within the range of life expectancy differences from county to county.

Housing Affordability (H+T)

Housing affordability has been one of the most persistent national concerns mainly because housing costs are the biggest expenses in the budgets of most households. A typical American household spends more than a third of its budget

Table 8.3: Direct, Indirect, and Total Effects of the County Compactness Index and Other Variables on Life Expectancy

	index	white	pop	SES	crime	crash	AQI90	BMI
direct effect	0.04	0.009	0	0.057	−0.008	−0.01	0	−0.036
indirect effect	−0.007	0.013	0	0.01	0	0	0	0
total effect	0.033	0.022	0	0.067	−0.008	−0.01	0	−0.036

Relationship of Sprawl to Topical Outcomes

on housing while poor and near-poor households commonly devote about half of their incomes to housing.

The majority of studies of housing affordability focus on housing cost and its relationship to household income as the sole indicator of affordability. The main providers of affordability indexes in the U.S. are real estate institutes and government agencies. The National Association of Realtors (NAR), for example, publishes a Housing Affordability Index for existing single-family homes by metropolitan area. The NAR Affordability Index measures whether or not a typical family could qualify for a mortgage loan on a typical home:

- A typical home is defined as the median-priced, existing single-family home as calculated by NAR.
- The typical family is defined as one earning the median family income as reported by the U.S. Bureau of the Census.
- The prevailing mortgage interest rate is the effective rate on loans closed on existing homes from the Federal Housing Finance Board.

These components are used to determine if the median income family can qualify for a mortgage on a typical home. Note that transportation costs associated with different development patterns are not factored into this calculation.

Likewise, the U.S. Department of Housing and Urban Development (HUD) has a standard of affordability that focuses exclusively on housing costs. If the ratio of housing costs to household income is less than 30 percent, then the dwelling is considered affordable (Belsky et al. 2005; HUD 2006). HUD's standard of affordability is the very definition of housing affordability (Linneman and Megbolugbe 1992; Belsky et al. 2005). The HUD measure is the legislative standard used to qualify applicants for housing assistance. It is used in the administration of rental housing subsidies, such as the Section 8 housing vouchers (Bogdon and Can 1997). In addition to qualifying ratios, it is often used to describe housing markets not only in the U.S. but also internationally (Robinson et al. 2006).

Both indices and standards are structurally flawed in that they only consider costs directly related to housing, ignoring those related to utilities and transportation. We know from the Consumer Expenditure Survey that the typical American household spends about 26.3 percent of income on housing, excluding utilities and public services costs. For the typical household, therefore, housing is affordable. But the typical household also spends 16.7 percent for transportation. Housing plus transportation costs consume 43 percent of household income in 2011. If a household's transportation costs were zero but

Relationship of Sprawl to Topical Outcomes

its housing costs were 35 percent of income, we would say that its housing was unaffordable, when in fact the household would be no worse off than the typical American household.

At the same time, previous studies show that there is a clear tradeoff between the housing and transportation expenses of working families. Families that spend more than half of their total household expenditures on housing put 7.5 percent of their budget towards transportation. By contrast, families that spend 30 percent or less of their total budget on housing spend nearly one-quarter of their budget on transportation—three times as much as those in less affordable housing (Dietz 1993; Lipman 2006).

The inherent weaknesses of traditional measures of housing affordability were revealed by the subprime mortgage crisis and ensuing wave of foreclosures that swept the U.S. in the late 2000s and directly helped precipitate the global financial crisis and the "Great Recession." Under traditional metrics of affordability, lenders granted loans to families who were unable to maintain mortgage payments, in many cases because of the crushing costs of transportation in an environment of record high motor vehicle fuel prices. Foreclosures were centered in the Sunbelt states of Arizona and Nevada, where rapid suburban and exurban development occurred in automobile dependent areas with virtually no transit access.

Addressing this issue, the Center for Neighborhood Technology (CNT) and the Center for Transit Oriented Development (CTOD) in 2006 developed an innovative tool that measured true housing affordability called the "Housing + Transportation Affordability Index." The H+T Affordability Index took into account not only the cost of housing, but also the intrinsic value of location, as quantified through transportation costs (Center for Transit-Oriented Development and Center for Neighborhood Technology 2006).

The H+T Affordability Index built on the analysis and theory of the location efficient mortgage (LEM), a lending product that was developed by a group of researchers for Fannie Mae in 2000. The LEM was rolled out in three regions. The LEM was very similar to the H+T Affordability Index in that it combined the costs of housing and transportation, and presumed that homebuyers could afford a bigger mortgage if they choose a neighborhood near public transit where they could realize significant savings on transportation (Holtzclaw et al. 2002).

Later in 2010–13, the Departments of Transportation and Housing and Development funded the development of a refined H+T-like index, called the Location Affordability Index (LAI). The LAI is based on the same methodology as H+T Affordability Index but uses the most recent and better quality data with more coverage.[2]

In the LAI, total housing costs are computed as current housing sales prices and rents from the American Community Survey, and household transportation costs are estimated at the census block group level for three separate cost components: costs of auto ownership, auto use, and transit use. Auto use is modeled based on household VMT data from Chicago and St. Louis. Auto ownership is modeled based on vehicle ownership data from the American Community Survey. Transit use and associated costs are based on Google transit feeds. Housing is considered affordable if the sum of housing and transportation costs is no more than 45 percent of household income.

Conceptual Framework

Our hypothesis is that urban sprawl can affect housing affordability in two ways. The first one is directly through the price of land and hence housing. The second is indirectly through the availability of transportation choices and the amount of driving people do. In this section we account for both effects, first individually and then together. We posit that due to higher land costs, compact areas will have more expensive housing. However, due to the availability of alternative modes and the shortness of auto trips, compact areas should entail lower transportation costs. *A priori*, it is impossible to say what the net effect of sprawl on housing + transportation costs will be. Instead, we approach the subject empirically in the subsections that follow.

Method

Data and Variables

Our variables and data sources are shown in Table 8.4. Our data relate to approximately 150,000 census block groups in 212 metropolitan areas and divisions. Most of the variables have been discussed and used before. The new ones are the three housing variables in Table 8.4: median year when housing units were built, percentage of vacant housing units, and percentage of owner-occupied housing units.

Analytical Method

Once again, the data used in this analysis are nested and must be analyzed accordingly. Census block groups form Level 1 in our nesting structure. Metropolitan areas, within which census block groups fall, form Level 2. Since

Relationship of Sprawl to Topical Outcomes

Table 8.4: Variables Used to Explain Housing + Transportation Affordability (variables log transformed)

Variables		Data Sources
Level 1 Dependent variables (block group level)		
hcost	housing costs as a percentage of income	LAI2013
tcost	transportation costs as a percentage of income	LAI2013
h+tcost	housing and transportation costs as a percentage of income	LAI2013
Level 1 Independent variables (block group level)		
hhsize	average household size	Census 2010
hhinc	median household income	ACS 2007–2011
pctwhite	percentage of white population	Census 2010
ybuilt	median year housing units built	ACS 2007–2011
pctvac	percentage of vacant housing units	ACS 2007–2011
pctown	percentage of owner-occupied housing units	ACS 2007–2011
Level 2 Independent Variables (metropolitan level)		
metpop	metropolitan area population	Census 2010
index	metropolitan compactness index for 2010	Computed in Chapter 7

all block groups located in an MSA share characteristics of that MSA such as metropolitan population size, we can say that block groups are "nested" within MSAs. Whenever individuals or other entities are "nested" within higher-level units, hierarchical or multilevel modeling (MLM) methods are preferred for explaining individual outcomes in terms of both individual and group characteristics. Multilevel modeling overcomes the limitations of OLS, accounting for the dependence among lower level units and producing more accurate coefficient and standard error estimates. So MLM is used in this analysis. Models were estimated with HLM 6.08.

Results

Results for simple housing affordability conform to our expectations (see Table 8.5). The block group average percentage of income spent on housing increases with median household income, percentage of whites in the population, the median year in which housing was built, and the percentage of housing which is owner occupied. The percentage of income spent on housing declines with

Relationship of Sprawl to Topical Outcomes

Table 8.5: Relationships to Housing Affordability (log-log form with robust standard errors)

	coeff.	t-ratio	p-value
constant	−13.39	−5.93	<0.001
hhsize	0.0052	0.183	0.855
hhinc	0.17	23.19	<0.001
pctwhite	0.012	2.744	0.007
ybuilt	1.79	5.937	<0.001
pctown	0.14	14.16	<0.001
pctvac	−0.0094	−2.53	0.012
metpop	0.019	2.097	0.037
index	0.113	4.108	<0.001
pseudo-R2		0.356	

the percentage of vacant units, as vacancies depress housing prices both directly by increasing supply relative to demand and indirectly by having negative spillover effects. Among Level 2 variables, housing affordability is greater in small than large metropolitan areas. That is a simple reflection of land prices and bid rent curves.

Controlling for these variables, the average percentage of income spent on housing is greater in compact than sprawling areas. This is to be expected. From the NAR Housing Affordability Index and common knowledge, housing is most expensive in the most compact metropolitan areas such as the New York and San Francisco areas. Each percent increase in the metropolitan compactness index is associated with a 0.11 percent increase in housing costs relative to income.

Results for transportation affordability are less intuitive (see Table 8.6). Unlike housing expenditures, LAI transportation expenditures are a modeled result, which may have introduced error. The block group average percentage of income spent on transportation increases with household size, median household income, and percentage of whites in the population. The relationship to household size is surprising, since larger households can make more efficient use of vehicles through carpooling and trip chaining. Among Level 2 variables, transportation affordability is greater in large than small metropolitan areas. This is also surprising since large areas are known to generate longer trips. Apparently, this effect is more than offset (in the LAI models) by greater availability of alternatives to the automobile and, correspondingly, lower automobile ownership in large areas.

Relationship of Sprawl to Topical Outcomes

Table 8.6: Relationships to Transportation Affordability (log-log form with robust standard errors)

	coeff.	t-ratio	p-value
constant	5.23	24.70	<0.001
hhsize	0.27	7.583	<0.001
hhinc	0.079	8.368	<0.001
pctwhite	0.042	7.713	<0.001
metpop	−0.13	−14.77	<0.001
index	−0.34	−10.31	<0.001
pseudo-R2		0.404	

Controlling for these variables, the average percentage of income spent on transportation is smaller in compact than sprawling areas. This is to be expected due to shorter trips and more transportation options in compact areas. Each percent increase in the metropolitan compactness index is associated with a 0.35 percent decrease in transportation costs relative to income.

The final analysis relates the sum of housing + transportation costs, again relative to income, to the same set of variables (see Table 8.7). The sum increases with household size, income, and other variables already discussed. This implies that other expenditures, such as food, utilities, and health care, actually decline in relation to income, as these variables increase. Most interesting, the sum of housing + transportation costs declines with metropolitan area compactness, though the relationship is significant only at the 0.10 level. This means that the decline in transportation costs with greater compactness more than offsets the rise in housing costs. This is a novel finding, conditioned only on quality of data upon which the LAI is based.

Upward Mobility

This American ideal is rooted in the Declaration of Independence: hard work is enough to create upward mobility, with greater opportunities, personal security, and affluence. But is the American ideal equally achievable for all societal groups?

Recent studies show that the U.S., as the land of opportunity for all, has one of the lowest rates of upward mobility in the developed world. Only a few citizens leave the class into which they are born for a higher one (DeParle 2012.). Downward mobility also is just as common as upward mobility,

Relationship of Sprawl to Topical Outcomes

Table 8.7: Relationships to Housing + Transportation Affordability (log-log form with robust standard errors)

	coeff.	t-ratio	p-value
constant	−24.26	−15.14	<0.001
hhsize	0.073	5.938	0.003
hhinc	0.102	19.86	<0.001
pctwhite	0.022	5.938	<0.001
ybuilt	3.56	16.36	<0.001
pctown	0.135	14.21	<0.001
pctvac	0.0083	3.997	<0.001
metpop	−0.031	−4.357	<0.001
index	−0.034	−1.790	0.074
pseudo-R2		0.427	

particularly for African Americans, but also for the middle class in general. In the U.S., a person born in the lowest economic class has only about a 2 percent chance of ending life anywhere near the top (Mazumder 2003; Jäntti et al. 2006).

Social mobility is an often-researched topic with scholarly articles on the subject dating back to the 1950s and 1960s. Much of the research has focused on race (Hardaway and McLoyd 2008), family background (Jäntti et al. 2006; Black and Devereux 2010), income (Corak 2006), and family structure, particularly divorce (DeLeire and Lopoo 2010) as determinants of social mobility. Poorly staffed and funded schools in poor and working-class neighborhoods, inadequate prenatal nutrition and health care, environmental hazards and pollution are some of the factors that affect the success of a poor youth seeking a better life (Delgado 2007).

Equality of Opportunity Project

A study of upward mobility by a team from Harvard and UC Berkeley made the news some time ago. Their study is appropriately titled "The Equality of Opportunity Project." They found that one of the key determinants of social mobility is geography; where a person grows up may dictate how likely that person is to move out of the social class into which he or she was born (Chetty et. al. 2013):

Relationship of Sprawl to Topical Outcomes

children from families at the 25th percentile in Seattle have outcomes comparable to children from families at the median in Atlanta. Some cities—such as Salt Lake City and San Jose—have rates of mobility comparable to countries with the highest rates of relative mobility, such as Denmark. Other cities—such as Atlanta and Milwaukee—have lower rates of mobility than any developed country for which data are currently available.

(Chetty et al. 2014a)

Chetty et al. (2014a) also state "intergenerational mobility varies substantially across areas within the U.S. For example, the probability that a child reaches the top quintile of the national income distribution starting from a family in the bottom quintile is 4.4% in Charlotte but 12.9% in San Jose."

What struck us immediately about these findings is a possible connection to sprawl. In our metropolitan rankings, Atlanta and Charlotte are at the sprawling end of the scale, while Salt Lake City and San Jose are far more compact. Metropolitan sprawl may contribute to the low rates of upward mobility for lower-income classes in sprawling metropolitan areas. The most important indicator of sprawl is poor accessibility (Ewing 1997). Considering the fact that those with low incomes have limited transportation mobility, inaccessibility of job opportunities could affect their ability to get ahead. Other causal pathways may also exist between sprawl and upward mobility (see below).

Chetty and colleagues (2014a) tested for correlations between upward mobility and possible causal factors (computing bivariate correlations). They caution that all of their findings are correlational and cannot be interpreted as causal effects. But they do find strong correlations between upward mobility and six factors:

- Income growth—Commuting zones (analogous to metropolitan areas) with low levels of income growth have low rates of upward mobility
- Racial segregation—Commuting zones with high levels of racial segregation have low rates of upward mobility
- Income inequality—Commuting zones with high levels of income inequality have low rates of upward mobility
- Quality of K–12 schools—Commuting zones with poor schools have low rates of upward mobility
- Social capital—Commuting zones with low levels of social capital (poor social networks and low community involvement) have low rates of upward mobility

- Family structure—Commuting zones with high levels of single parenting have low rates of upward mobility

Chetty and colleagues also speculate on a link between sprawl and upward mobility. They operationalize sprawl in terms of commute times to work, but that is as far as they go: "we also find that upward mobility is higher in cities with less sprawl, as measured by commute times to work" (Chetty et al. 2014b). As we have shown in this book, there are much better ways to measure sprawl than "commute times to work." Indeed, some of the most compact metropolitan areas have some of the longest commute times, by virtue of their size and heavy use of transit (which typically involves longer travel times than automobiles). Think New York City and San Francisco.

Job Inaccessibility

After World War II, many wealthy Americans decentralized out of the cities and into the suburbs. Shopping and support services followed them, leaving poor and minority populations behind. In 1968, John Kain formulated the spatial mismatch hypothesis, speculating that poor black workers left in central cities were increasingly distant from and poorly connected to major centers of growth. They were constrained by discrimination in labor and housing markets and central city job shortages. The spatial mismatch hypothesis has implications for inner city residents that are dependent on low-level entry jobs. Distance from work centers can lead to increasing unemployment rates among inner-city residents and increased poverty outcomes for the region as a whole.

Commuting cost is one obstacle to inner-city workers landing jobs in the suburbs. Autos may be too expensive for low-income workers, and public transportation is problematic in the sense that it is not always reliable and may not stop at all job sites. Information access to jobs may also hinder matches between inner-city workers and suburban jobs. People who are living away from the job center are generally less knowledgeable about potential openings than individuals who live closer to the job center. Therefore, networking and information spillovers are of major advantage in accessing information about potential openings.

There were many empirical studies on the spatial mismatch hypothesis in the early 1970s, soon after the hypothesis was advanced by Kain. There was resurgent interest in the hypothesis in the early 1990s, when at least six review articles were published (Jencks and Mayer 1990; Wheeler 1990; Moss and Tilly 1991; Holzer 1991; Kain 1992; Ihlanfeldt 1994).

Relationship of Sprawl to Topical Outcomes

Recently, Horner and Mefford (2007) analyzed conditions for spatial mismatch controlling for race, ethnicity, and the mode of commuting. The results revealed how potential commute options differ across commuter groups and how minority job–housing alternatives are more spatially constrained (Horner and Mefford 2007). The analysis confirmed that minority residential and employment patterns differ from their non-minority counterparts, and these differences manifest themselves in a more spatially restricted pattern of residential location.

While the focus is different, the concept of jobs–housing balance is related to spatial mismatch. Jobs–housing balance requires a match-up between the skill level of local residents and local job opportunities as well as between the earnings of workers and the cost of local housing (Cervero 1989). The imbalance occurs because some parts of the metropolitan area are job rich and housing poor, others are housing rich and job poor, and few provide both residences and employment sites for roughly an equal number of people (Cervero 1989).

A study by Cervero (1989) explained the underlying factors that affect the jobs–housing balance in communities. Four main factors were apparent. First, the practice of zoning land predominantly for high-revenue-generating and low-services-demanding land uses has limited the supply of housing in many areas and driven housing prices upward (Rolleston 1987). Second, due to fiscal zoning and restriction of housing supplies, many moderate-salaried service industry workers cannot afford the single-family homes located in the suburbs. Many workers are priced out of the housing market and are forced to live farther from employment locations. Many suburban areas, moreover, are experiencing serious labor shortages; increasingly, businesses are finding it necessary to operate special shuttles to transport inner-city residents to such job sites as hotels and fast-food restaurants (Cervero 1989). Third, the trend toward multiple wage-earner households has also contributed to jobs–housing imbalances. Where there is a clear distinction between primary and secondary wage earners, most households could be expected to locate closer to the workplace of the primary wage earner, with the secondary wage earner commuting (Cervero 1989). Lastly, jobs–housing balance is influenced by the increasing rate of job turnover compared to past generations.

Many studies have been conducted analyzing the imbalance of jobs to housing and how that affects commuting times. Cervero and Duncan (2006) conducted a study that related VMT to jobs–housing balance and retail–housing mix. Using best-fitting regression models they were able to isolate the effects on VMT of accessibility variables and control variables. The results of the study show that linking jobs and housing holds a significant potential to reduce VMT. Cervero and Duncan (2006) suggest that "achieving jobs-housing balance is one of the most important ways land-use planning can contribute to reducing motorized travel." Similarly, Sarzynski et al. (2006) examined the influences of seven dimensions of land use in 1990 on subsequent changes in commute times in 2000 for a sample of 50 large U.S. urban areas. They found that housing–job proximity was the only built-environment variable negatively and significantly associated with commute time.

Social Capital

The majority of studies on the relationship between sprawl on social capital have focused on factors such as trust and neighborhood ties (Freeman 2001; Leyden 2003; Lund 2003; Brueckner and Largey 2006; Nguyen 2010). In his 2001 study, Freeman successfully established a negative relationship between the level of car usage and the level of social ties in neighborhoods. Leyden (2003) found that high neighborhood walkability resulted in a higher likelihood of establishing relationships with one's neighbors, general social interaction, and political participation. Lund (2003) tested New Urbanist claims that placing amenities such as parks and retail shops within walking distance of homes will increase pedestrian travel and thereby increase interaction among neighbors.

Meanwhile, researchers continue to debate the benefits of compact development, and some have demonstrated that social capital is not diminished by suburban sprawl. Brueckner and Largey (2006), for example, regressed individuals' social-interaction variables on census-tract density in a study using the Social Capital Benchmark Survey data. Their analysis showed that high density had a negative effect on all friendship and group-involvement variables.

Most recently, Nguyen (2010) related our earlier county compactness/sprawl index to social-capital factors from the Social Capital Community Benchmark Survey. This study found that urban sprawl may support some types of social capital while negatively affecting the others. So the evidence on the effects of sprawl on social capital is clearly mixed, but it certainly could represent a pathway between sprawl and upward mobility.

In this study we use the social capital index (SCI) from the Chetty et al. database (2014a) as the measure of social capital. It was originally measured by Rupasingha and Goetz (2008) and employed by Putnam (2007). This index is comprised of voter turnout rates, the fraction of people who return their census forms, and various measures of participation in community organizations in the area.

Relationship of Sprawl to Topical Outcomes

Racial Segregation

The evidence regarding sprawl's impact on racial segregation is mixed. Some studies point to the cost of housing/land as the primary contributors to black–white residential segregation. Kahn (2001) has shown that, controlling for household income and metropolitan patterns of racial segregation, sprawl was significant in closing the gap between black and white rates of suburban homeownership between 1980 and 1990. In other words, sprawling metropolitan areas provide greater opportunities for suburban homeownership by black households. The study also found that blacks are more likely to own larger homes in sprawling regions. This is said to be a direct result of more affordable housing in sprawling metropolitan areas.

Galster and Cutsinger (2007) analyzed the relationship between land-use patterns and levels of black and white segregation in 50 U.S. metropolitan areas. They found a direct correlation between sprawl and desegregation. They surmised that "the dominant relationship observed is that, on several measures, more sprawl-like land use patterns are associated with less segregation" (Galster and Cutsinger 2007). They identified the land/housing price effect as the dominant mechanism through which land-use patterns influence black and white segregation measures.

By contrast, Nelson et al. (2004) found that urban containment measures were effective at reducing black and white segregation levels in designated metropolitan areas between 1990 and 2000. Urban containment measures can be assumed to reduce the degree of sprawl in a region.

In this study, racial segregation is represented by black isolation. The variable comes from the Chetty et. al. (2013) study for commuting zones and is computed based on Census 2000 data.

Income Segregation

A final possible causal pathway between sprawl and upward mobility is income segregation. Income segregation is related to spatial mismatch and racial segregation, but is operationalized differently. Margo (1992) argues that the movement of metropolitan populations in the U.S. toward suburban locales over the latter half of the 20th century can be linked, to a significant degree, to the rise in personal incomes. As individual incomes rose, so did the demand for land. As a result, higher-income households moved to the outskirts, while lower-income households remained within central cities.

Relationship of Sprawl to Topical Outcomes

According to Jargowsky (2002) this movement of higher-income households isolated those in the central cities, leading to concentrations of poverty and a lack of resources, such as employment and educational opportunities. Furthermore, he argues that "these spatial disparities increase poverty in the short run and reduce equality of opportunity, therefore contributing to inequality in the long run" (Jargowsky 2002).

Wheeler (2006) conducted a statistical analysis inquiring if urban decentralization and income inequality were associated. The study found an inverse relationship between urban density and the degree of income inequality within metropolitan areas, suggesting that, as cities spread out, they become increasingly segregated by income.

A study by Reardon and Bischoff (2011) investigated how the growth in income inequality from 1970 to 2000 affected patterns of income segregation along three dimensions: the spatial segregation of poverty and affluence, race-specific patterns of income segregation, and the geographic scale of income segregation. The analysis yielded four findings:

- Increasing income inequality was responsible for 40–80 percent of the changes in income segregation from 1970–2000.
- Income inequality affects income segregation primarily by affecting the segregation of affluence rather than the segregation of poverty.
- Income inequality and income segregation differs for black and white families. The study relates this to housing policies and housing discrimination seen throughout the last half century.
- Income inequality appears to increase income segregation largely by inducing the highest-earning families to move far away from lower-income households.

In this analysis, the segregation of poverty, as a proxy for income segregation, is borrowed from Chetty et al. (2013) and is defined as the extent to which individuals in the bottom quartile are segregated from those above the bottom quartile.

Data and Measures

We used data on upward mobility and covariates from the Equality of Opportunity databases of Chetty et al. (2013; 2014a), but added a sprawl metric from our own study (see Table 8.8). The measure of upward mobility we chose to use was the probability that a child born to a family in the bottom quintile

Relationship of Sprawl to Topical Outcomes

of the national income distribution reached the top quintile of the national income distribution by age 30. That is the third of three measures quantified in their study, and is highly correlated with the first measure, what they call relative mobility, which is defined as the difference in the expected economic outcomes between children from high-income and low-income families. We chose the third measure because it is simple to interpret.

Our exogenous variables (that drive the system) are the rate of income growth between 2000 and 2010, the share of families with kids with a female head of

Table 8.8: Variables Used to Explain Upward Mobility

Variables		Data sources
Endogenous variables		
upward	The probability that a child born to a family in the bottom quintile of the national income distribution in 1980–1982 reaches the top quintile of the national income distribution in 2010–2011	EOP 2013
socialcap	Index of social capital that aggregates various measures identified by Putnam and collaborators	Rupasingha and Goetz (2008); EOP 2013
blackiso	Geographic Isolation of Blacks (Cutler, Glaeser, Vigdor isolation index). Computed as the difference between the average share of black residents in a black person's neighborhood and the total share of black residents in the CZ, normalized to fall between zero and one	EOP 2013
povseg	Measure of how evenly those in the lower-income quartile are distributed across census tracts within a CZ. This is Thiel's H measure for the two groups defined by splitting the population at the national 25th percentile of income	EOP 2013
Exogenous variables		
incgrowth	Annualized growth rate (2000–2008) in real household income per working age capita (16–64)	EOP 2013; Census 2000; ACS 2010
gini	Computed by EOP team using parents of children in the core sample, with income top coded at $100 million in 2012 dollars	EOP 2013
femkids	Share of families with kids with a female householder and no husband	EOP 2013; Census 2000
stratio	Average student-teacher ratio in public schools	EOP 2013
index	Metropolitan compactness index for 2010	Computed in Chapter 7

household and no husband in 2000, the mean student–teacher ratio in 1996, and the metropolitan compactness/sprawl index for 2010. We would expect that upward mobility is positively related to the rate of income growth, school spending, and the compactness index, and negatively related to the share of female–headed families.

Regarding our metropolitan compactness index for 2010, we would have preferred using an index for a year near the midpoint of the 30-year period over which upward mobility manifests itself, but did not have such an index. Fortunately, from our longitudinal analysis of urbanized area sprawl in Chapter 9, urban form does not change dramatically from decade to decade. Our compactness index is also for metropolitan areas rather than commuting zones as defined by Chetty et al. Commuting zones include rural counties and sometimes more than one metropolitan area. In the latter case, we computed weighted averages of the compactness/sprawl index, weighting by population. Because boundaries of commuting zones and metropolitan areas are not coincident, we dropped commuting zones from our sample if their populations differed from the combined metropolitan areas by more than 25 percent. It is unfortunate that we lost observations in this manner, but we still had a sample of 122 commuting zones from which to estimate our models.

Analytical Methods

We used SEM to estimate both direct and indirect effects of urban sprawl on upward mobility. We estimated our SE model of upward mobility with Amos 19.0 and maximum likelihood procedures. We analyzed data for 122 metropolitan areas and divisions that had no missing data.

As suggested by the literature, we included three plausible causal pathways connecting sprawl indirectly with upward mobility—one through social capital, a second through income segregation, and a third through racial segregation. The fourth pathway between sprawl and upward mobility is direct, most likely reflecting job accessibility, spatial mismatch, and jobs–housing balance.

Model and Results

We have estimated a structural equation model of upward mobility. The model is shown in Figure 8.2. We included three plausible causal pathways connecting sprawl indirectly with upward mobility – one through social capital, a second through income segregation, and a third through racial segregation. A fourth pathway between sprawl and upward mobility is direct, most likely reflecting job accessibility, spatial mismatch, and jobs-housing balance. Maximum likelihood methods were used in the estimations. Model evaluation was based on four factors: (1) theoretical soundness; (2) chi-square tests of absolute model fit; (3) root-mean-square errors of approximation (RMSEA), which unlike the chi-square, correct for sample size; and (4) comparative fit indices (CFI).

Direct relationships are presented in Table 8.9. Relationships are mostly significant and as expected. Goodness-of-fit measures at the bottom of the table suggest that the model provides a good fit to the data (see Chapter 5 for a discussion of these measures). The upward mobility model in Figure 8.2 has a chi-square of 1.9 with 6 model degrees of freedom and a p-value of 0.93. The low chi-square relative to model degrees of freedom and a high (>0.05) p-value are indicators of good model fit.

The metropolitan compactness index has a strong direct relationship to upward mobility, plus indirect relationships through two mediating variables. The direct relationship seems to be capturing some phenomenon that is missed

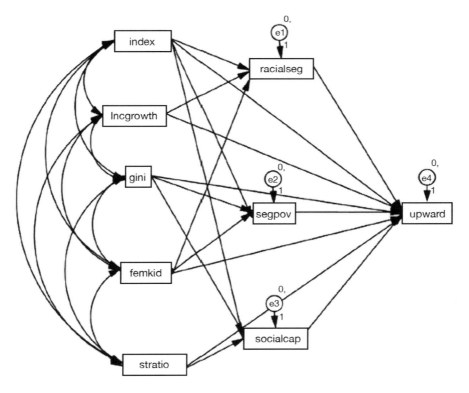

Figure 8.2: Causal Path Diagram for Upward Mobility in Terms of Metropolitan/Commuting Zone Compactness and Other Variables

Relationship of Sprawl to Topical Outcomes

Table 8.9: Direct Effects of Variables on One Another in the Upward Mobility Model

			coefficient	std error	p-value
socialcap	<—	index	0.188	0.071	0.014
racialseg	<—	index	0.019	0.079	0.742
racialseg	<—	femkid	0.447	0.052	0.009
sepgov	<—	femkid	0.306	0.097	0.005
racialseg	<—	ingrowth	−0.214	0.069	0.011
sepgov	<—	index	0.182	0.081	0.012
sepgov	<—	gini	0.109	0.091	0.167
socialcap	<—	gini	−0.647	0.061	0.013
socialcap	<—	stratio	−0.211	0.064	0.006
upward	<—	racialseg	−0.04	0.074	0.4
upward	<—	sepgov	−0.156	0.056	0.008
upward	<—	incgrowth	0.345	0.056	0.004
upward	<—	femkid	−0.467	0.065	0.019
upward	<—	socilacap	−0.032	0.106	0.907
upward	<—	stratio	0.146	0.069	0.009
upward	<—	gini	0.003	0.093	0.864
upward	<—	index	0.308	0.071	0.005
chi-square	1.9 degree of freedom=6 p-value=0.93				
RMSEA	0 p-value=0.97				
CFI	1.00				

by the mediating variables. The obvious phenomenon is better accessibility of low-income people to employment opportunities in compact areas. Let's consider each indirect effect in turn. The compactness index is inversely related to racial segregation, but not at a significant level. The compactness index is directly related to both social capital and poverty segregation. Of these two variables, poverty segregation has a significant negative relationship to upward mobility, as expected, while social capital has no relationship to upward mobility.

Of the other exogenous variables in the model, income growth is positively related to upward mobility, while the share of female-headed households with kids is negatively related to upward mobility. Both income growth and female-headed families have indirect relationships to upward mobility through the

Relationship of Sprawl to Topical Outcomes

mediating variable, racial segregation. Income growth adds to upward mobility indirectly, while female–headed families detract from upward mobility indirectly. The Gini coefficient, which represents income inequality, is unrelated to upward mobility. The student–teacher ratio, which relates to school quality, is positively related to upward mobility, a largely unexpected result (though not entirely, see Gladwell, 2013).

Direct, indirect, and total effects of variables on one another are shown in Table 8.10. The net indirect effect of compactness on upward mobility is negative due to the increase in income segregation that accompanies compactness. However, the indirect effect of compactness through the mediating variable is small compared to the direct effect of compactness on upward mobility. Using upward mobility data from a credible source, and a validated compactness/sprawl index, we conclude that upward mobility is significantly higher in compact than sprawling metropolitan areas/commuting zones. The point elasticity of upward mobility with respect to compactness is 0.41. As the compactness index doubles (increases by 100 percent), the likelihood that a child born into the bottom fifth of the national income distribution will reach the top fifth by age 30 increases by about 41 percent. For the average poor kid in our sample, with an 8 percent chance of moving up into the top quintile, this represents an increase of 3.2 percent in absolute terms, well within the range of upward mobility differences from metropolitan area to metropolitan area. The extreme values in our sample are a 2.6 per cent chance of upward mobility in Memphis, TN, and 14.0 per cent in Provo, UT.

Our results are generally consistent with those of Chetty et al. (2013, 2014a), who looked at simple correlations between upward mobility and seven potential causal factors: income growth, family structure, school quality, racial segregation, poverty segregation, social capital, and sprawl (represented by commute times). However, we have gone a step further than Chetty et al., measuring sprawl explicitly, controlling for confounding influences, and then examining both direct and indirect causal pathways between sprawl, as measured, and upward

Table 8.10: Direct, Indirect, and Total Effects of the Metropolitan Compactness Index and Other Variables on Upward Mobility

	racialseg	sepgov	incgrowth	femkid	Socialcap	stratio	gini	index
Direct effect	–0.04	–0.156	0.345	–0.467	–0.032	0.146	0.003	0.308
Indirect effect	0	0	0.009	–0.066	0	0.007	0.004	–0.035
Total effect	–0.04	–0.156	0.353	–0.533	–0.032	0.153	0.007	0.273

mobility. The direct effect, which we attribute to better job accessibility in more compact commuting zones, is stronger than the indirect effects. We can tentatively add greater upward social and economic mobility, longer life expectancy, and greater housing + transportation affordability, to the many other benefits of compact development.

Notes

1   See: www.healthmetricsandevaluation.org/publications/summaries/left-behind-widening-disparities-males-and-females-us-county-life-expectancy-#/data-methods. Accessed February 5, 2016.
2   See: www.locationaffordability.info/. Accessed February 5, 2016.

References

Belsky, E.S., Goodman, J., and Drew, R. (2005). Measuring the nation's rental housing affordability problems. The Joint Center for Housing Studies, Harvard University. Available online at: www.jchs.harvard.edu/publications/rental/rd051_measuring_rental_affordability05.pdf (last accessed 5 May 2017).

Bereitschaft, B., and Debbage, K. (2013). Urban form, air pollution, and CO_2 emissions in large U.S. metropolitan areas. *The Professional Geographer*, 65(4), 612–635.

Black, S.E., and Devereux, P.J. (2010). *Recent Developments in Intergenerational Mobility*. National Bureau of Economic Research, Working Paper 15889. Available online at: www.nber.org/papers/w15889.pdf?new_window=1 (last accessed 5 May 2017).

Bogdon, A.S., and Can, A. (1997). Indicators of local housing affordability: Comparative and spatial approaches. *Real Estate Economics*, 25(1), 43–60.

Browning, C.R., Byron, R.A., Calder, C.A., Krivo, L.J., Kwan, M.P., Lee, J.Y., and Peterson, R.D. (2010). Commercial density, residential concentration, and crime: Land use patterns and violence in neighborhood context. *Journal of Research in Crime and Delinquency*, 47(3), 329–357.

Brueckner, J., and Largey, A. (2006). *Social Interaction and Sprawl*. Working Paper 060707, Department of Economics, University of California, Irvine, CA.

Center for Transit-Oriented Development and Center for Neighborhood Technology (2006). *The Affordability Index: A New Tool for Measuring the True Affordability of a Housing Choice*. Brookings Institution, Washington, D.C.

Cervero, R. (1989). Jobs-housing balancing and regional mobility. *Journal of the American Planning Association*, 55(2), 136–150.

Cervero, R., and Duncan, M. (2006). Which reduces vehicle travel more: Jobs-housing balance or retail-housing mixing? *Journal of the American Planning Association*, 72(4), 475–490.

Chetty, R., Hendren, N., Kline, P., and Saez, E. (2013). *Economic Impacts of Tax Expenditures: Evidence from Spatial Variation Across the U.S.* The Equality of Opportunity Project. Available online at: www.irs.gov/pub/irs-soi/14rptax expenditures.pdf (last accessed 11 May 2017).

Chetty, R., Hendren, N., Kline, P., and Saez, E. (2014a). *Where is the Land of Opportunity? The Geography of Intergenerational Mobility in the United States.* National Bureau of Economic Research, Washington D.C.

Chetty, R., Hendren, N., Kline, P., and Saez, E. (2014b). Where is the Land of Opportunity? Intergenerational Mobility in the U.S., VOX CEPR's Policy Portal. Available online at: http://voxeu.org/article/where-land-opportunity-intergenerational-mobility-us (last accessed 5 May 2017).

Christenson, B., and Johnson, N. (1995). Educational inequality in adult mortality: An assessment with death certificate data from Michigan. *Demography*, 32, 215–229.

Corak, M. (2006). Do poor children become poor adults? Lessons from a cross-country comparison of generational earnings mobility. In Creedy, J., and Kalk, G. (Eds) *Dynamics of Inequality and Poverty* (pp. 143–188). Emerald Group Publishing Limited, Bradford.

DeLeire, T., and Lopoo, L.M. (2010). *Family Structure and the Economic Mobility of Children.* The Pew Charitable Trusts: Economic Mobility Project. Available online at: www.pewstates.org/uploadedFiles/PCS_Assets/2010/Family_Structure.pdf (last accessed 5 May 2017).

Delgado, R. (2007). The myth of upward mobility. *University of Pittsburgh Law Review*, 68(4), 879–913.

DeParle, J. (2012). Harder for Americans to rise from lower rungs. *New York Times*, 4 January. Available online at: www.nytimes.com/2012/01/05/us/harder-for-americans-to-rise-from-lower-rungs.html (last accessed 5 May 2017).

Dietz, R. (1993). A joint model of residential and employment location in urban areas. *Journal of Urban Economics*, 44, 197–215.

Dockery, D.W. (2009). Health effects of particulate air pollution. *Annals of Epidemiology*, 9(4), 257–263.

Doyle, S., Kelly-Schwartz, A., Schlossberg, M., and Stockard, J. (2006). Active community environments and health: The relationship of walkable and safe communities to individual health. *Journal of the American Planning Association*, 72(1), 19–31.

Elo, I., and Preston, S. (1996). Educational differentials in morality: United States, 1979–85. *Social Science and Medicine*, 42, 47–57.

Ewing, R. (1997). Is Los Angeles-style sprawl desirable? *Journal of the American Planning Association*, 63(1), 107–126.

Ewing, R., Pendall, R., and Chen, D. (2002). *Measuring Sprawl and Its Impacts.* Smart Growth America, Washington, D.C.

Ewing, R., Pendall, R., and Chen, D. (2003a). Measuring sprawl and its transportation impacts. *Transportation Research Record*, 1832: 175–183.

Ewing, R., Schieber, R., and Zegeer, C. (2003b). Urban sprawl as a risk factor in motor vehicle occupant and pedestrian fatalities. *American Journal of Public Health*, 93, 1541–1545.

Ezzati, M., Friedman, A., Kulkarni, S., and Murray, C. (2008). The reversal of fortunes: Trends in county mortality and cross-county mortality disparities in the United States. *PLoS Medicine*, 5(4), 557–568.

Fan, Y., and Song, Y. (2009). Is sprawl associated with a widening urban–suburban mortality gap? *Journal of Urban Health: Bulletin of the New York Academy of Medicine*, 86(5), 708–728.

Freeman, L. (2001). The effects of sprawl on neighborhood social ties: An explanatory analysis. *Journal of American Planning Association*, 67(1), 69–77.

Galster, G., and Cutsinger, J. (2007). Racial settlement and metropolitan land-use patterns: Does sprawl abet black-white segregation? *Urban Geography*, 28(6), 516–553.

Gladwell, M. (2013). *David and Goliath: Underdogs, misfits, and the art of battling giants.* Little, Brown and Company, New York.

Hardaway, C.R., and McLoyd, V.C. (2008). Escaping poverty and securing middle class status: How race and socioeconomic status shape mobility prospects for African Americans during the transition to adulthood. *Journal of Youth and Adolescence*, 38(2), 242–256.

Holcombe, R.G., and Williams, D.W. (2012). Urban sprawl and transportation externalities. *The Review of Regional Studies*, 40(3), 257–272.

Holtzclaw, J., Clear, R., Dittmar, H., Goldstein, D., and Haas, P. (2002). Location efficiency: Neighborhood and socio-economic characteristics determine auto ownership and use-studies in Chicago, Los Angeles and San Francisco. *Transportation Planning and Technology*, 25(1), 1–27.

Holzer, H.J. (1991). The spatial mismatch hypothesis: What has the evidence shown? *Urban Studies*, 28, 105–122.

Horner, M.W., and Mefford, J.N. (2007). Investigating urban spatial mismatch using job-housing indicators to model home-work separation. *Environment and Planning A*, 39(6), 1420.

HUD (U.S. Department of Housing and Urban Development) (2006). *Housing Impact Analysis*. U.S. Government Printing Office, Washington, D.C. Available online at: www.huduser.gov/Publications/pdf/hsgimpact.pdf (last accessed 5 May 2017).

Ihlanfeldt, K. (1994). The spatial mismatch between jobs and residential locations within urban areas. *Cityscape*, 1(1), 219–244.

Jäntti, M., Bratsberg, B., Røed, K., Raaum, O., Naylor, R., Osterbacka, E., Bjorklund, A., and Eriksson, T. (2006). *American Exceptionalism in a New Light: A comparison of intergenerational earnings mobility in the Nordic countries, the United Kingdom and the United States,* IZA Discussion Paper No. 1938.

Jargowsky, P.A. (2002). Sprawl, concentration of poverty, and urban inequality. In Squires, G. (Ed.) *Urban Sprawl: Causes, consequences and policy response* (pp. 39–72). Urban Institute Press, Washington, D.C.

Jencks, C., and Mayer, S.E. (1990). Residential segregation, job proximity, and black job opportunities. In Lynn, Jr., L.E., and McGreary, M.M. (Eds) *Inner-City Poverty in the United States* (pp. 187–222). National Academic Press, Washington, D.C.

Johnson, R., and Wolinsky, F. (1993). The structure of health status among older adults: Disease, disability, functional limitation, and perceived health. *Journal of Health and Social Behavior*, 34, 105–121.

Kahn, M.E. (2001). Does sprawl reduce the black/white housing consumption gap? *Housing Policy Debate*, 12(1), 77–86.

Kahn, M.E. (2006). *Green Cities: Urban growth and the environment*. Brookings Institution Press, Washington, D.C.

Kain, J.F. (1992). The spatial mismatch hypothesis: Three decades later. *Housing Policy Debate*, 3(2), 371–462.

Kelly-Schwartz, A., Stockard, J., Doyle, S., and Schlossberg, M. (2004). Is sprawl unhealthy? A multilevel analysis of the relationship of metropolitan sprawl to the health of individuals. *Journal of Planning Education and Research*, 24, 184–196.

Kim, D., Subramanian, S.V., Gortmaker, S.L., and Kawachi, I. (2006). U.S. state- and county-level social capital in relation to obesity and physical inactivity: a multilevel, multivariable analysis. *Social Science & Medicine*, 63(4), 1045–1059.

Kneebone, E. (2009). *Job Sprawl Revisited: The Changing Geography of Metropolitan Employment*. Metro Economy Series for the Metropolitan Policy Program at Brookings, Brookings Institution, Washington D.C.

Kneebone, E., and Raphael, S. (2011). *City and Suburban Crime Trends in Metropolitan America*. Brookings Institution Metropolitan Policy Program, Washington, D.C.

Kochanek, K.D., Xu, J., Murphy, S.L., Miniño, A.M., and Kung, H.C. (2011). National vital statistics reports. *National Vital Statistics Reports*, 59(4), 1.

Kochanek, K.D., Arias, E., and Anderson, R.N. (2013). How did cause of death contribute to racial differences in life expectancy in the United States in 2010. *NCHS Data Brief*, 125, 1–8.

Kostova, D. (2011). Can the built environment reduce obesity? The impact of residential sprawl and neighborhood parks on obesity and physical activity. *Eastern Economic Journal*, 37(3), 390–402.

Lee, I.M., Ewing, R., and Sesso, H.D. (2009). The built environment and physical activity levels: The Harvard Alumni Health Study. *American Journal of Preventive Medicine*, 37(4), 293–298.

Levy, J.I., Carrothers, T.J., Tuomisto, J.T., Hammitt, J.K., and Evans, J.S. (2001). Assessing the public health benefits of reduced ozone concentrations. *Environmental Health Perspectives*, 109(12), 9–20.

Leyden, K. (2003) Social capital and built environment: The importance of walkable neighborhood. *American Journal of Public Health*, 93(9), 1546–1551.

Linneman, P.D., and Megbolugbe, I.F. (1992). Housing affordability: Myth or reality? *Urban Studies*, 29(3), 369–392.

Lipman, B.J. (2006). *A Heavy Load. The Combined Housing and Transportation Burdens of Working Families.* Technical report prepared for Center for Housing Policy, Washington, D.C.

Litman, T. (2013). Safer than you think! Revising the transit safety narrative. *Journal of Public Transportation.* Available online at: www.vtpi.org/safer.pdf (last accessed 5 May 2017).

Lucy, W.H. (2003). Mortality risk associated with leaving home: Recognizing the relevance of the built environment. *American Journal of Public* Health, 93(9), 1564–1569.

Lund, H. (2003). Testing the claims of New Urbanism: Local access, pedestrian travel, and neighboring behaviors. *Journal of the American Planning Association*, 69(4), 414–429.

Margo, R.A. (1992). Explaining the postwar suburbanization of population in the United States: The role of income. *Journal of urban economics*, 31(3), 301–310.

Mazumder, B. (2003) *Revised Estimates of Intergenerational Income Mobility in the United States.* Federal Reserve Bank of Chicago Working Paper 2003-16, Chicago, IL.

Mirowsky, J., and Ross, C. (2000). Socioeconomic status and subjective life expectancy. *Social Psychology Quarterly*, 63(2), 133–151.

Mokdad, A.H., Marks, J.S., Stroup, D.F., and Gerberding, J.L. (2004). Actual causes of death in the United States, 2000. *Journal of the American Medical Association*, 291(10), 1238–1245.

Moss, P., and Tilly, C. (1991). *Why Black Men Are Doing Worse in the Labor Market.* Social Science Research Council, New York.

Myers, S.R., Branas, C.C., French, B.C., Nance, M.L., Kallan, M.J., Wiebe, D.J., and Carr, B.G. (2013). Safety in numbers: Are major cities the safest places in the United States? *Annals of Emergency Medicine*, 62(4), 408–418.

Nelson, A.C., Sanchez, T.W., and Dawkins, C.J. (2004). The effect of urban containment and mandatory housing elements on racial segregation in U.S. metropolitan areas, 1990–2000. *Journal of Urban Affairs*, 26(3), 339–350.

Nguyen, D. (2010). Evidence of the impacts of urban sprawl on social capital. *Environment and Planning B: Planning and Design*, 37(4), 610–627.

Olshansky, S.J., Passaro, D.J., Hershow, R.C., Layden, J., Carnes, B.A., Brody, J., and Ludwig, D.S. (2005). A potential decline in life expectancy in the United States in the 21st century. *The New England Journal of Medicine*, 352(11), 1138–1145.

Plantinga, A., and Bernell, S. (2007). The association between urban sprawl and obesity: Is it a two-way street? *Journal of Regional Science*, 47(5), 857–879.

Putnam, R.D. (2007). *E pluribus unum*: Diversity and community in the twenty-first century. The 2006 Johan Skytte Prize Lecture. *Scandinavian Political Studies*, 30(2), 137–174.

Reardon, S.F., and Bischoff, K. (2011). Income inequality and income segregation 1. *American Journal of Sociology*, 116(4), 1092–1153.

Redelings, M., Lieb, L., and Sorvillo, F. (2010). Years off your life? The effects of homicide on life expectancy by neighborhood and race/ethnicity in Los Angeles county. *Journal of Urban Health*, 87(4), 670–676.

Reynolds, J., and Ross, C. (1998). Social stratification and health: Education's benefit beyond economic status and social origins. *Social Problems*, 45, 221–247.

Robinson, M., Scobie, G.M., and Hallinan, B. (2006). Affordability of housing: Concepts, measurement and evidence. *MONTH*, 6, 04.

Rogers, R. (1992). Living and dying in the USA: Sociodemographic determinants of death among blacks and whites. *Demography*, 29, 287–304.

Rolleston, B.S. (1987). Determinants of restrictive suburban zoning: An empirical analysis. *Journal of Urban Economics*, 21(1), 1–21.

Ross, C., and Wu, C. (1995). The links between education and health. *American Sociological Review*, 60, 719–745.

Rupasingha, A., and Goetz, S.J. (2008). *U.S County-Level Social Capital Data, 1990–2005*. The Northeast Regional Center for Rural Development, Penn State University, University Park, PA.

Sarzynski, A., Wolman, H.L., Galster, G., and Hanson, R. (2006). Testing the conventional wisdom about land use and traffic congestion: The more we sprawl, the less we move? *Urban Studies*, 43(3), 601–626.

Schweitzer, L., and Zhou, J. (2010). Neighborhood air quality outcomes in compact and sprawled regions. *Journal of the American Planning Association,* 76(3), 363–371.

Shaw, J., Horrace, W., and Vogel, R. (2005). The determinants of life expectancy: An analysis of the OECD health data. *Southern Economic Journal,* 71(4), 768–783.

Silva, R.A., West, J.J., Zhang, Y., Anenberg, S.C., Lamarque, J.F., Shindell, D.T., and Zeng, G. (2013). Global premature mortality due to anthropogenic outdoor air pollution and the contribution of past climate change. *Environmental Research Letters,* 8(3), 034005.

Stone, B. (2008). Urban sprawl and air quality in large U.S. cities. *Journal of Environmental Management,* 86, 688–698.

Stone, B., Hess, J., and Frumkin, H. (2010). Urban form and extreme heat events: Are sprawling cities more vulnerable to climate change than compact cities? *Environmental Health Perspectives,* 118(10), 1425–1428.

Sturm, R., and Cohen, D. (2004). Suburban sprawl and physical and mental health. *Public Health,* 118(7), 488–496.

Trowbridge, M.J., Gurka, M.J., and O'Connor, R. (2009). Urban sprawl and delayed ambulance arrival in the United States. *American Journal of Preventive Medicine,* 37(5), 428–432.

Wang, H., Schumacher, A.E., Levitz, C.E., Mokdad, A.H., and Murray, C.J. (2013). Left behind: Widening disparities for males and females in U.S. county life expectancy, 1985–2010. *Population Health Metrics,* 11(1), 8.

Wassmer, R.W., and Baass, M.C. (2006). Does a more centralized urban form raise housing prices? *Journal of Policy Analysis and Management,* 25(2), 439–462.

Wheeler, C.H. (2006). *Urban Decentralization and Income Inequality: Is Sprawl Associated with Rising Income Segregation Across Neighborhoods?* Federal Reserve Bank of St. Louis Working Paper Series, (2006-037), St. Louis, MO.

Wheeler, L.A. (1990). *A Review of the Spatial Mismatch Hypothesis: Its Impact on the Current Plight of Central City in the United States.* Occasional paper no. 137. Metropolitan Studies Program, The Maxwell School of Citizenship and Public Affairs, Syracuse University, Syracuse, N.Y.

World Health Organization (2003). *Health Aspects of Air Pollution with Particulate Matter, Ozone and Nitrogen Dioxide.* Report on a WHO working group, Bonn, Germany, 13–15 January.

Zolnik, E.J. (2011). The effect of sprawl on private-vehicle commuting outcomes. *Environment and Planning A,* 43(8), 1875–1893.

Chapter Nine

Urbanized Areas: A Longitudinal Analysis

In this chapter we seek to measure changes in sprawl by developing refined and enhanced compactness/sprawl indices for 2000 and 2010 based on definitions and procedures in Ewing et al. (2002; 2003), but refined and applied this time to urbanized areas (UZAs) rather than metropolitan areas or counties. We chose census UZAs as our units of analysis because UZAs are the only census geographies that expand systematically with urban development over time. Counties have fixed boundaries and hence tend to appear more compact over time (except when counties are losing population as in Detroit or New Orleans after Katrina). Metropolitan areas expand in large increments as entire counties, both urban and rural portions, are added to core counties to reflect changing commuting patterns and social and economic integration.

Census UZAs expand incrementally as rural areas are converted to urban uses and density thresholds are exceeded. If expansion takes the form of low densities, segregated land uses, commercial strips, and poorly connected streets, compactness scores will decrease. Conversely, if expansion occurs with moderate to high densities, integrated land uses, activity centers, and interconnected streets, compactness scores will increase. Likewise, if growth occurs though infill and redevelopment, compactness scores will increase.

This chapter uses principal component analysis (PCA) and 2010 cross-sectional data for large U.S. UZAs to operationalize compactness/sprawl in each of four dimensions: development density, land-use mix, activity centering, and street connectivity. Higher values represent greater compactness, lower values greater sprawl. The four factors are then combined into an overall compactness/sprawl index.

The chapter then applies factor score coefficient values for 2010 to the same variables for 2000 to create comparable metrics for 2000. Compactness scores

143

Urbanized Areas: A Longitudinal Analysis

for 2000 are compared to the same scores for 2010 to see which UZAs sprawled the most between censuses, and which sprawled the least or actually became more compact.

Finally, the chapter validates the compactness index and its component factors against transportation outcomes for 2010, specifically walk mode share, transit mode share, and average drive time on the journey to work. We then seek further validation by relating changes in compactness between 2000 and 2010 to changes in commuting outcomes. This is a much more stringent test of association/causation, since changes over a decade are small compared to sampling errors associated with commuting data from the American Community Survey. Also, in a time-step analysis, we can only hope to capture short-term effects of compactness on commuting, whereas cross-sectional analyses capture long-term effects. Not surprisingly, results of the longitudinal analysis are disappointing.

Methods

Sample

The term "urbanized area "as defined by the U.S. Census Bureau denotes an urban area of 50,000 or more people. Urban areas are defined by core census block groups or blocks with population densities of at least 1,000 people per square mile and surrounding census blocks with densities of at least 500 people per square mile. Urbanized areas often provide a more accurate gauge of city size than do the incorporated political boundaries of cities.

This investigation is limited to large urbanized areas. Our sample consists of the 162 largest urbanized areas in the U.S., those with more than 200,000 population in 2010. The rationale for thus limiting our sample is simple: the concept of sprawl has particular relevance to large areas where the economic, social, and environmental consequences of sprawl can be significant. The concept of sprawl does not have much relevance to small urbanized areas such as Pine Bluff, AR and Monroe, MI.

Variables

In all, we have measured 15 variables in four dimensions for 162 urbanized areas in both 2000 and 2010.

Urbanized Areas: A Longitudinal Analysis

Development Density

Our first four density variables are the same as in the original county sprawl index, gross density of urban and suburban census tracts (popden), percentage of the population living at low suburban densities (lt1500), percentage of the population living at medium to high urban densities (gt12500), and urban density based on the National Land Cover Database (urbden). The fifth density variable (empden) is analogous to the first, except it is derived with employment data from the LED database rather than population data. In this case, LED data were processed for the years 2005 and 2010. Year 2005 is the earliest year that LED data are available for all states (except Massachusetts). The data were aggregated from census block geography to census block group geography to generate total jobs by two-digit NAICS code for every block group in the nation.

Land-Use Mix

Although using the same variables as Ewing et al. (2002) to operationalize mixed use, we computed them differently using one-mile buffers around the centers of block groups rather than computing them within the boundaries of block groups. The reason is that measures of mixed use are sensitive to the size of a block group. The smaller the area is, the lower the job–population balance is expected to be, because small areas are usually homogeneous and the majority of them contain only employment or population. Also the larger the area is, the higher the value of entropy because the block group will contain more jobs. By using a uniform one-mile buffer, we make the unit of analysis comparable for all block groups.

The two mixed-use variables were calculated for each block group's buffer using block-level population data from the 2010 Census, and block-level employment data from the 2010 LED database. The resulting job and population totals were used to compute a job–population balance measure (jobpop). This variable equals one for block groups with the same ratio of jobs-to-residents within the one-mile ring as the urbanized area as a whole; zero for block groups with only jobs or residents within the one-mile ring, not both; and intermediate values for intermediate cases. All values were weighted by the sum of block group jobs and residents as a percentage of the UZA total.

For the second mixed-use variable, each block group centroid was again buffered with a one-mile ring, and jobs by sector were summed for blocks within the ring. An entropy formula was then used to compute a measure of job mix (jobmix). The variable equals one for block groups with equal numbers of jobs in each sector within the ring; zero for block groups with all jobs in a single sector within the ring; and intermediate values for intermediate cases. The sectors considered in this case were retail, entertainment, health, education, and personal services. Values were weighted by the sum of block group population and employment as a percentage of the urbanized areas total.[1]

Unlike the mixed-use factors at the county and metropolitan levels, the mixed-use factor at the urbanized area level does not include a third variable, Walk Score. The reason is simple. This is a longitudinal comparison of sprawl in 2000 and 2010, and Walk Score data were not available until 2007.

Activity Centering

Centering is the compactness dimension with the most significant improvement compared to Ewing et al.'s earlier indices, as we identified not only CBDs but also employment subcenters nationwide as a part of this study. Ewing et al. (2002) measured metropolitan centering in terms of concentrations of employment in or around (within three miles) historic CBDs of metropolitan areas, and at a considerable distance from (more than 10 miles) from historic CBDs. This way of measuring centering does not make much sense when applied to small urbanized areas because almost all of the jobs and population fall within three miles of CBDs. It also doesn't make sense in large polycentric metropolitan areas, where historic CBDs have sometimes been eclipsed by edge cities.

The first centering variable came straight out of Ewing et al. (2002; 2003) and the 2010 Census. It is the coefficient of variation in census block group population densities, defined as the standard deviation of block group densities divided by the average density of block groups (varpop). The more variation in population densities around the mean, the more centering and/or subcentering exists within the urbanized areas.

The second centering variable is analogous to the first, except it is derived with employment data from the LED database. It is the coefficient of variation in census block group employment densities, defined as the standard deviation of block group densities divided by the average density of block groups (varemp). The more variation in employment densities around the mean, the more centering and/or subcentering exists within the urbanized areas.

Ewing et al. (2002) used a 1980 shapefile as published by Census Bureau to identify CBDs. The shapefile identified the location of CBDs only for 232 of the largest metropolitan areas. The shapefile is now more than 30 years old and

Urbanized Areas: A Longitudinal Analysis

does not capture new CBDs that have emerged since 1980. Moreover, large subcenters are found in virtually all large metropolitan areas of today, and the existence of and proximity to these are what distinguish polycentric urban areas.

The next two centering variables measure the proportion of employment and population within CBDs and employment subcenters. We first identified the location of CBDs and employment subcenters for all metropolitan areas (see Chapter 3). Using this procedure, we found 224 metropolitan areas to be monocentric (have only one center), 132 to be polycentric (have more than one center), and 18 metropolitan areas to have no CBD or subcenter. This procedure resulted in two new centering variables as the percentage of UZA population (popcen) and employment (empcen) in CBDs and subcenters.

Street Connectivity

Street connectivity is related to block size since smaller blocks translate into shorter and more direct routes. Large block sizes indicate a relative paucity of street connections and alternate routes. So, two street accessibility variables were computed for each urbanized area: average block size (avgblk) and percentage of blocks with areas less than 1/100 square mile, the size of a typical traditional urban block bounded by sides just over 500 feet in length (smlblk).

These two variables were part of Ewing et al.'s original sprawl metrics. To them, we have added two new variables. They are intersection density and percentage of four-or-more way intersections.

For each UZA, the total number of intersections in the UZA was divided by the land area to obtain intersection density (intden), while the number of four-or-more-way intersections was multiplied by 100 and divided by the total number of intersections to obtain the percentage of four-or-more way inter-sections (4-way).

Statistical Methods

In this chapter we use two statistical methods. Principal component analysis (a type of factor analysis) is used to derive individual compactness indices that represent the built environments of UZAs. Then linear regression analysis is used to relate these indices to transportation outcomes, controlling for influences other than the built environment.

For each dimension of sprawl, principal components were extracted from the component variables. The principal component selected to represent the dimension was the one capturing the largest share of common variance among

Urbanized Areas: A Longitudinal Analysis

the component variables, that is, the one upon which the observed variables loaded most heavily. Because, in this study, the first component captured the majority of the combined variance of these variables, no subsequent components were considered.

The other statistical method used in this study is linear regression (ordinary least squares or OLS). Our dependent variables were logged so as to be normally distributed and hence properly modeled with regression analysis. As for the independent variables (control variables), we transformed all variables into log form to achieve a better fit with the data, reduce the influence of outliers, and adjust for nonlinearity of the data. The transformations have the added advantage of allowing us to interpret regression coefficients as elasticities. An elasticity is a percentage change in one variable that accompanies a 1 percent change in another variable. Elasticities are the most common measures of effect size in both economics and planning.

Results

Individual Compactness/Sprawl Factors

Factor loadings (that is, correlations of these variables with each factor), eigenvalues, and percentages of explained variance are shown in Table 9.1. The eigenvalue of the density factor is 3.82, which means that this one factor accounts for almost as much of the total variance in the datasets as four component variables combined, more than three quarters of the total variance. As expected, one of the variables loads negatively on the density factor, that being the percentage of population living at less than 1,500 persons per square mile. The rest load positively. Thus, for all component variables, higher densities translate into higher values of the density factor.

The eigenvalue of the mix factor is 1.54, which means that this one factor accounts for more than three quarters of the total variance in the dataset. Both component variables load positively on the mix factor.

The eigenvalue of the centering factor is 2.20, which means that this one factor accounts for just over half of the total variance in the datasets. All component variables load positively on the centering factor.

The eigenvalue of the street factor is 2.75, which means that this one factor accounts for two thirds of the total variance in the dataset. As expected, one of the variables loads negatively on the street connectivity factor, that being the average block size. The rest load positively. Thus, for all component variables, more street connectivity translates into higher values of the street factor.

Table 9.1: Variable Loadings on Four Factors for 2010

Component matrix		Data sources	2010 Factor loadings
Density factor			
popden	gross population density	Census 2010	0.970
empden	gross employment density	LED 2010	0.891
lt1500	percentage of the population living at low suburban densities	Census 2010	−0.806
gt12500	percentage of the population living at medium to high urban densities	Census 2010	0.745
urbden	net population density of urban lands	NLCD	0.941
Eigenvalue			3.82
Explained variance			76.5%
Mix factor			
jobpop	Job–population balance	LED 2010	0.879
jobmix	degree of job mixing (entropy)	LED 2010	0.879
Eigenvalue			1.54
Explained variance			77.2%
Centering factor			
varpop	coefficient of variation in census block group population densities	Census 2010	0.661
varemp	coefficient of variation in census block group employment densities	LED 2010	0.749
popcen	percentage of UZA population in CBD or subcenters	Census 2010	0.757
empcen	percentage of UZA employment in CBD or subcenters	LED 2010	0.790
Eigenvalue			2.20
Explained variance			54.8%
Street factor			
smlblk	percentage of small urban blocks	Census 2010	0.844
avgblksze	average block size	Census 2010	−0.947
intden	intersection density	TomTom 2007	0.726
4way	percentage of four-or-more-way intersections	TomTom 2007	0.784
Eigenvalue			2.75
Explained variance			68.8%

Urbanized Areas: A Longitudinal Analysis

Overall Compactness/Sprawl Index for 2010

Some of the technical literature on sprawl includes size in the definition. Certainly, sheer geographic size is central to popular notions of sprawl. Despite their relatively high densities, urbanized areas such as Los Angeles and Phoenix are perceived as sprawling because they "go on forever." A sprawl index that disregarded this aspect of urban form would never achieve face validity.

Accordingly, we sought a method of transforming the sum of the four sprawl factors into a sprawl index that would be neutral with respect to population size. In this study, we use the exact same procedure used with metropolitan area sprawl in the early 2000s (Ewing et al. 2002; 2003). The transformation was accomplished by regressing the sum of the four sprawl factors on the natural logarithm of the population of the urbanized area. The standardized residuals (difference between actual and estimated values divided by the standard deviation of the difference) became our overall measure of sprawl. Given the way it was derived, this index is uncorrelated with the log of population. Urbanized areas that are more compact than expected, given their population size, have positive values. Urbanized areas that are more sprawling than expected, again given their population size, have negative values. This adjustment for population size still leaves the sprawl index highly correlated with the sum of the four component factors (r = 0.87).

As with the individual sprawl factors, we transformed the overall sprawl index (index) into a metric with a mean of 100 and a standard deviation of 25. This was done for the sake of consistency and ease of understanding. With this transformation, the more compact urbanized areas have index values above 100, while the more sprawling have values below 100. Table 9.2 presents overall compactness scores and individual component scores for the 10 most compact and the 10 most sprawling large urbanized areas. By these metrics, San Francisco is the most compact large urbanized area, and Atlanta is the most sprawling.

Overall Compactness/Sprawl Index for 2000

To make apples to apples comparisons between two years (2000 and 2010), we applied the factor coefficient matrices for four principal components in 2010 to built environmental variable values for 2000. This resulted in compactness factors for 2000 that are consistent with those for 2010.

Table 9.3 presents overall compactness scores and component scores for the 10 most compact and the 10 most sprawling large urbanized areas in 2000. As one would expect, rankings did not change dramatically in most cases over the

Urbanized Areas: A Longitudinal Analysis

Table 9.2: Compactness/Sprawl Scores for 10 Most Compact and 10 Most Sprawling UZAs in 2010

Rank		comfac	denfac	mixfac	cenfac	strfac
10 most compact UZAs						
1	San Francisco-Oakland, CA	180.94	205.69	129.92	164.34	153.38
2	Reading, PA	169.32	127.71	150.87	124.45	147.46
3	Madison, WI	152.87	118.16	121.82	182.19	99.33
4	Eugene, OR	152.54	114.84	134.37	134.15	123.07
5	Laredo, TX	151.80	123.87	131.21	81.56	166.54
6	Oxnard, CA	146.19	147.55	137.14	82.42	135.08
7	Atlantic City, NJ	144.25	93.87	91.07	157.06	143.86
8	Los Angeles-Long Beach-Anaheim, CA	143.42	212.21	144.75	102.23	138.92
9	Lincoln, NE	143.38	118.63	127.46	97.02	141.77
10	New York-Newark, NY-NJ-CT	142.71	197.50	106.80	179.10	125.06
10 most sprawling UZAs						
153	Baton Rouge, LA	64.38	81.92	75.30	77.21	77.61
154	Fayetteville, NC	61.05	79.40	73.65	67.16	64.43
155	Chattanooga, TN-GA	60.96	68.92	54.18	97.03	70.33
156	Greenville, SC	60.57	67.92	75.26	89.88	57.88
157	Nashville-Davidson, TN	60.27	87.51	47.43	111.18	70.03
158	Charlotte, NC-SC	57.41	82.95	64.56	115.94	53.01
159	Winston-Salem, NC	55.56	66.31	68.97	88.15	54.29
160	Victorville-Hesperia, CA	54.15	82.38	67.79	57.01	61.88
161	Hickory, NC	48.64	46.92	78.41	72.20	44.94
162	Atlanta, GA	37.45	84.64	75.63	107.29	36.84

10 years. San Francisco was the most compact in 2000, and has remained so. Atlanta was the most sprawling in 2000, and has remained so.

Validation Against Transportation Outcomes

The relationships between sprawl and travel outcomes can be used to validate the urbanized area sprawl measures. If sprawl has any consistently recognized outcome, it is automobile dependence. We would expect to find that, after controlling for other relevant influences, compact urbanized areas have relatively high transit and walking commute mode shares and short drive times to work.

Urbanized Areas: A Longitudinal Analysis

Table 9.3: Compactness/Sprawl Scores for 10 Most Compact and 10 Most Sprawling UZAs in 2000

Rank		comfac	denfac	mixfac	cenfac	strfac
10 most compact UZAs						
1	San Francisco-Oakland, CA	184.06	219.66	128.39	162.41	149.84
2	Laredo, TX	174.12	134.65	148.02	86.2	189.55
3	Reading, PA	155.74	119.44	157.15	126.12	118.53
4	Eugene, OR	151.42	121.5	141.47	130.73	114.89
5	New Orleans, LA	149.64	161.24	106.84	95.97	181.06
6	Stockton, CA	147.55	134.42	145.18	104.41	124.09
7	Madison, WI	147.2	122.06	126.86	158.37	101.3
8	Visalia, CA	145.05	116.84	142.48	107.53	108.93
9	New York-Newark, NY-NJ-CT	141.75	197.18	115.6	170.57	120.19
10	Lincoln, NE	141.19	118.03	133.12	97.15	135.15
10 most sprawling UZAs						
153	Fayetteville, NC	64.13	85.50	99.95	108.27	35.77
154	Baton Rouge, LA	61.39	78.97	98.97	62.63	56.65
155	Palm Bay-Melbourne, FL	58.18	83.46	72.66	85.07	64.16
156	Nashville-Davidson, TN	58.11	76.29	75.93	62.16	77.64
157	Victorville-Hesperia, CA	55.43	89.26	67.83	106.22	46.10
158	Winston-Salem, NC	53.49	74.79	84.24	56.75	51.04
159	Bonita Springs, FL	52.49	66.67	68.56	93.67	44.02
160	Chattanooga, TN-GA	49.7	76.78	77.85	61.38	46.22
161	Hickory, NC	48.76	65.83	55.21	92.30	53.90
162	Atlanta, GA	39.5	49.14	81.34	75.33	42.67

Table 9.4 provides a list of all dependent and independent variables used in the validation. With American Factfinder, we downloaded data from the 2010 ACS five-year estimates, and computed walk and transit mode shares and average drive times for census urbanized areas. From the 2010 Census, we downloaded data on gender, age, race, household size, and computed percentages and mean values to describe urbanized area populations.

We estimated two sets of regression models. Our first set of regressions used the overall compactness index for 2010 (index) as an independent variable. The second set of regressions used the four compactness/sprawl factors individually

Urbanized Areas: A Longitudinal Analysis

Table 9.4: Variables Used to Explain Travel Outcomes (all variables log transformed)

Variables		Data Sources
Dependent variables		
walkshr	percentage of commuters walking to work	ACS 2007–2011
transitshr	percentage of commuters using public transportation (excluding taxi)	ACS 2007–2011
drivetime	average journey-to-work drive time in minutes	ACS 2007–2011
Independent variables		
pop	urbanized area population	Census 2010
hhsize	average household size	Census 2010
age1524	percentage of population 15–24 years old	Census 2010
male	percentage of male population	Census 2010
white	percentage of white population	Census 2010
income	income per capita	ACS 2007–2011
fuel	average fuel price for the metropolitan area	OPIC 2010
index	urbanized areas compactness index for 2010	computed
denfac	density factor (a weighted combination of five density variables)	Census 2010, NLCD database
mixfac	mix factor (a weighted combination of two mixed-use variables)	Census 2010, LED database
cenfac	centering factor (a weighted combination of four centering variables)	Census 2010, Claritas
strfac	street factor (a weighted combination of four street-related variables)	Census 2010, TomTom, ESRI

(denfac, mixfac, cenfac, strfac) as independent variables. Both sets of regressions included control variables.

Also, in both sets of regressions, the dependent variables were logged so as to be normally distributed and hence properly modeled with OLS regression. All independent variables were also transformed into log form to achieve a better fit with the data, reduce the influence of outliers, and adjust for nonlinearity of the data. The transformations had the added advantage of allowing us to interpret regression coefficients as elasticities.

Results for models with the overall compactness index are presented in Table 9.5. Control variables mostly have the expected signs and often are significant. The compactness index (index) has the expected strong positive relationships

Urbanized Areas: A Longitudinal Analysis

Table 9.5: Relationships of UZA Compactness Index in 2010 to Transportation Outcomes (log-log transformed – t-statistics in parentheses)

	walkshr	transitshr	drivetime
constant	2.44	–6.47	2.12
pop	0.13(3.80)***	0.42(7.706)***	0.033(3.11)**
hhsize	–1.21(-3.16)**	1.18(1.87)	0.89(7.19)***
age1524	1.16(8.18)***	0.86(3.68)***	–0.13(-2.79)**
male	–3.12(-1.74)	–7.33(-2.48) *	–0.92(-1.59)
white	0.45(2.66) **	0.17(0.62)	–0.084(-1.53)
income	0.065(0.31)	1.83(5.42)***	0.39(5.87)***
fuel	1.17(1.93)*	2.66(2.67)**	0.52(2.69)**
index	0.74(6.38)***	1.04(5.44)***	–0.12(-3.17)***
adjusted R2	0.53	0.62	0.61

* .05 probability level
** .01 probability level
*** .001 probability level

to walk and transit mode shares, and the expected negative relationship to average drive time. As noted, the coefficients of these log-log models are elasticities. For every percentage increase in the compactness index, the walk mode share increases by 0.74 percent, the transit mode share increases by 1.04 percent, and the average drive time declines by 0.12 percent. Based on these results, we declare the overall compactness index to be validated.

The new multidimensional compactness factors are mostly significant with the expected signs (see Table 9.6). The centering factor, cenfac, is the most important correlate of walking, followed by the mix factor, mixfac, and the density factor, denfac. The street factor has a negative sign but is not significant. The centering factor is also the most important correlate of transit use, followed by the density factor. The other two compactness factors are not significant. All of the compactness factors have negative signs in the drive time equation, but only the density factor is significant. We declare the density and centering factors to be validated. The mix factor has promise based on its correct sign and significance in the walk share equation. The street factor is never significant and has the opposite signs to what we expected. Given the fact that all four street variables load as expected on the street factor, we are confident that we properly operationalized street connectivity. But we have no explanation for the disappointing regression results.

Urbanized Areas: A Longitudinal Analysis

Table 9.6: Relationships of 2010 UZA Individual Compactness Factors to Transportation Outcomes (log-log transformed – t-statistics in parentheses)

	walkshr	transitshr	drivetime
constant	3.76	0.326	1.62
pop	–0.015(-.37)	0.16(2.23)*	0.056(3.94)***
hhsize	–0.93(-2.21)*	1.33(1.88)	0.99(6.86)***
age1524	0.89(5.78)***	0.41(1.59)	–0.094(-1.78)
male	–3.18(-1.85)	–8.74(-3.05)**	–0.904(-1.54)
white	0.46(2.83)**	0.29(1.08)	–0.087(-1.56)
income	–0.18(-.85)	1.50(4.28)***	0.43(5.96) ***
fuel	0.91(1.52)	2.39(2.39)*	0.64(3.09)**
denfac	0.53(2.03)*	1.33(3.05)***	–0.17(-1.92)*
mixfac	0.36(2.98)**	0.087(0.43)	–0.057(-1.38)
cenfac	0.79(6.05)***	1.06(4.93)***	–0.026(-0.59)
strfac	–0.08(-0.63)	–0.082(-0.37)	0.016(0.35)
adjusted R2	0.60	0.66	0.61

* .05 probability level
** .01 probability level
*** .001 probability level

Attempted Validation Using Change Variables

As noted in the introduction, a longitudinal analysis is a more stringent test of association/causation than is a cross-sectional analysis. In our longitudinal analyses, we related changes in compactness and socioeconomic variables between 2000 and 2010 to changes in commuting outcomes during the same time period. Such analyses control for unmeasured characteristics of urbanized areas that may confound results in cross-sectional analyses, but largely cancel out in longitudinal analyses.

If our compactness measures are valid, we would expect to see some change in transportation outcomes associated with a change in compactness measures for individual urbanized areas. However, we would expect much weaker relationships in longitudinal than cross-sectional analyses for two reasons: first, changes over a decade are small compared to sampling errors associated with commuting data from the ACS, and relatedly, we can only hope to capture short-term effects of compactness on commuting in a 10-year longitudinal analysis.

Urbanized Areas: A Longitudinal Analysis

We looked at changes in three commuting variables—walk mode share, transit mode share, and average drive time on the journey to work. The most significant relationship is between the change in the density factor and the change in the transit mode share ($p = <0.001$). The other significant relationship is between the change in the centering factor and the change in the transit mode share ($p = 0.014$). These relationships mirror those of the cross-sectional analysis. No other relationships proved significant in any of our models.

Discussion

This chapter developed and sought to validate an overall measure of compactness/sprawl for U.S. urbanized areas in 2010. It also sought to validate individual factors representing four dimensions of compactness/sprawl: development density, land-use mix, activity centering, and street connectivity. By these measures, San Francisco is the most compact urbanized area in the nation, and Atlanta is the most sprawling.

We were able to validate the overall index against transportation outcome measures, specifically walk mode share, transit mode share, and average drive time on the journey to work. We were also able to validate the factors representing density and centering. The factor representing land mix was less predictive of transportation outcomes, but did have a significant relationship to walking, as one would expect. Only the factor representing street accessibility could not be validated.

Once we had measures of compactness for 2010, we were able to apply the same factor coefficients to data for 2000, thus generating consistent measures of compactness for 2000 and allowing longitudinal comparisons. Generalizing across the entire universe of large urbanized areas, compactness decreased and sprawl increased between the two census years, but only slightly. Summing the four indices of compactness (each with an average score of 100 in 2010), the average combined score was 405.8 in 2000, dropping to 400 in 2010, a relatively small change. This means that that on average, urbanized areas became less compact between 2000 and 2010. However, the average case obscures some interesting stories.

Los Angeles saw an impressive rise in its compactness ranking, from 18th in 2000 to 8th in 2010. The reason: infill development. "Contradicting metropolitan L.A.'s reputation as the capital of unbridled sprawl, roughly two-thirds of new housing built there between 2005 and 2009 was infill – constructed in previously developed areas rather than on raw land in the exurbs" (Boxall 2012).

Urbanized Areas: A Longitudinal Analysis

New Orleans dropped seven places between 2000 and 2010, from 5th to 12th most compact, which is a result of population loss following Katrina. The drop would have been greater in the immediate aftermath of the hurricane. "The magnitude of population loss after Katrina ... means the city has needed to add relatively few people to rank among the fastest-growing places in the nation since 2007. It also has been aided by billions in federal reconstruction dollars and a healthy tourism industry" (Bass 2012).

Stockton was 6th most compact in 2000 and dropped to 16th in 2010. This is presumably due to the housing bubble, which burst in Stockton perhaps more than any other city in the nation. Stockton has been referred to as "Fore-closureville" due to its record high home foreclosure rate (Nieves 2010).

Charlotte rose from 11th most sprawling to 5th most sprawling during the decade, now competing to be the next Atlanta:

> A recent study by Northwest Environment Watch, a nonprofit research and communication center based in Seattle, shows Charlotte as having the worst urban sprawl out of 15 cities across the nation. Charlotte ranked last in every category, including land converted from rural area to suburban and urban areas, average metropolitan density and growth in compact neighborhoods.
> (Tompkins 2009)

So the compactness/sprawl measures have the additional quality of face validity. They paint a plausible picture of sprawl in the U.S.

Note

1   See "Land-use mix" section for the formula used for computing job–population balance and job–mix measures.

References

Bass, F. (2012). Katrina comeback makes New Orleans fastest-growing city. *Bloomberg*, 27 June. Available online at : www.bloomberg.com/news/2012-06-28/katrina-comeback-makes-new-orleans-fastest-growing-city.html (last accessed 5 May 2017).

Boxall, B. (2012). Infill housing development rises in Los Angeles region. *Los Angeles Times*, 20 December. Available onlineat: http://articles.latimes.com/2012/dec/20/science/la-sci-sn-infill-housing-increases20121220 (last accessed 5 May 2017).

Urbanized Areas: A Longitudinal Analysis

Ewing, R., Pendall, R., and Chen, D. (2002). *Measuring Sprawl and Its Impacts.* Smart Growth America, Washington, D.C.

Ewing, R., Pendall, R., and Chen, D. (2003). Measuring sprawl and its transportation impacts. Transportation *Research Record*, 1832, 175–183.

Nieves, E. (2010). Stockton, California is Foreclosureville, USA, has one of the worst foreclosure rates In the United States, *Huffington Post Business*, 10 January. Available online at: www.huffingtonpost.com/2010/01/10/stockton-california-is-fo_n_417704.html (last accessed 10 June 2014).

Tompkins, K. (2009). Charlotte sprawl among worst in country. *The Daily Tar Heel*, 22 August. Available online at: www.dailytarheel.com/article/2004/11/charlotte_sprawl_among_worst_in_country (last accessed 5 May 2017).

Chapter Ten

Case Examples for Planners

This study has updated county and metropolitan compactness/sprawl indices, widely used by planning and public researchers since their release in 2002 and 2003. The updated indices reflect conditions on the ground circa 2010.

This study has also developed new measures of compactness/sprawl that incorporate additional dimensions of the construct "sprawl," and used additional variables to operationalize these dimensions. The four dimensions, measured individually and with a composite index, are development density, land-use mix, activity centering, and street connectivity. Measures are immediately available to study the costs and benefits of different urban forms. They have been posted on an NIH website and are available for download (http://gis.cancer.gov/tools/urban-sprawl/).

Using updated and enhanced measures of compactness/sprawl, this study has validated both the original and new indices, and largely validated the individual measures representing the four dimensions of sprawl. These new results mirror and confirm the earlier findings of Ewing et al. (2002; 2003a; 2003b; 2003c). If anything, relationships of sprawl to important quality-of-life outcomes are stronger than in the original studies.

An obvious question is what does all of this mean for practicing planners. This chapter answers the question with case examples from different parts of the U.S. The following are examples of cities in metro areas that performed well in each of the four Index factors, and the public policies that contributed to their success.

Development Density: Los Angeles, CA

Los Angeles, CA had the second-highest density score in the country, topped

Case Examples for Planners

only by the New York metro area, an outlier nationally. Several public policies have contributed to Los Angeles' high development density score.

A Plan for Development Around Transit Stations

In 2012, Los Angeles' Department of City Planning began an initiative to create detailed plans for development surrounding 10 light rail stations. The Los Angeles Transit Neighborhood Plans project "aims to support vibrant neighborhoods around transit stations, where people can live, work and shop or eat out, all within a safe and pleasant walk to transit stations."[1]

Allowing Higher Density in Exchange for Affordable Housing

Los Angeles' Affordable Housing Incentives Ordinance gives developers the option to build up to 25 percent above the otherwise allowable residential density level if they include affordable housing in their project.[2] It also reduces the parking requirements and allows the development to go through an expedited approval process.

A Zoning Code for Los Angeles Today and Tomorrow

In 2013, Los Angeles began a multi-year process to update its zoning code, which was first drafted in 1946. This process is just at its beginnings but plans to have a new code in place by 2017. The new code will be web-based, easier to use and create a unified development code for projects downtown.

Land-Use Mix: Santa Barbara, CA

Santa Barbara, CA—the fourth most compact and connected metro area nationally—had the best score among small metro areas for its land-use mix. Several public policies have contributed to Santa Barbara's high land-use mix score.

Forward-Thinking Zoning Codes

The City of Santa Barbara's zoning codes allow residential uses in most commercial zones.[3] This is as a result of a public planning process in the 1990s that sought to create more affordable housing. This resulted in amendments to the General Plan and Zoning Ordinance that encouraged mixed-use developments in certain areas.[4] Now, mixed use is characteristic of Santa Barbara.

Case Examples for Planners

Encouraging Mixed Use in the General Plan

Not content to allow mixed use, the City of Santa Barbara also made this strategy a development priority by including it in the city's 2011 General Plan Update. The update outlined three Principles of Development, one of which is to "Encourage a mix of land uses to include: strong retail and workplace centers, residential living in commercial centers with easy access to grocery stores and recreation, connectivity and civic engagement, and public space for pedestrians."[5]

County-Level Support

Santa Barbara County, which encompasses the City of Santa Barbara, maintains community plans for unincorporated areas of the county. The County has established mixed use zones and encourages mixed use in many of the community plans in order to encourage a mix of uses throughout the county.[6]

Activity Centering: Madison, WI

The city of Madison, WI—the densest and most connected medium–sized metro area in the country—also had the highest score nationally for activity centering, meaning people and businesses are concentrated in downtown and subcenters. Several public policies have contributed to Madison's high activity centering score. Here are a few.

Homebuyer Assistance Programs

Madison has several programs that help residents purchase homes, many of which encourage residency downtown and reinvestment in existing housing stock.[7] One example is the Mansion Hill-James Madison Park Neighborhood Small Cap TIF Loan Program.[8] This program makes available 0 percent interest-forgivable second mortgage loans to finance a portion of the purchase price and the rehabilitation costs of a residential property located in the Mansion Hill-James Madison Park Neighborhood of downtown Madison.

A Comprehensive Focus on Downtown Development

In 1994, Madison adopted a series of Strategic Management System Goals, which outlined ways for Madison to "share in the growth that is occurring in

Case Examples for Planners

Dane County … in such a way to balance our economic, social and environmental health."[9] Directing new growth toward existing urban areas, increasing owner-occupied housing in the city, and creating economic development areas were all among the strategies recommended to achieve this. The goals later influences the City's 2006 comprehensive plan.[10]

Downtown Plan

In 2012 the City of Madison adopted a new Downtown Plan, which aims to strengthen Madison's downtown neighborhood. The plan includes nine strategies to guide the future growth of this core neighborhood while sustaining the traditions, history, and vitality that make Madison a model city.

Street Connectivity: Trenton, NJ

The street connectivity factor examines average block sizes, the percent of urban blocks that are small, the density of intersections and the percent of intersections that are four-way or more. Trenton, NJ—the seventh most compact, connected metro area nationally—had the highest score for street connectivity among all small and medium-sized metro areas. A number of public policies helped Trenton achieve its high street connectivity score.

A City Designed for People

Trenton is the historic center city of the larger metro area, and a number of small town centers surround it. This interconnected network of city and town centers encouraged reinvestment within the existing city grid.

Transportation Master Plan

Trenton's Transportation Master Plan focuses on maintaining the existing transportation network, using investments to support downtown, and supporting multimodal options for all the neighborhoods. A walkable city has, by definition, small blocks and frequent intersections. The plan also places a high priority on key objectives to reach these goals, such as: improve and maintain the city's transit infrastructure, encourage transit-supportive land uses, and avoid increases in street capacity unless addressing a critical transportation problem.

Case Examples for Planners

Investing in transportation

Greater Trenton has a long history of investing in transportation. In 1870, Trenton was the first place to lay asphalt on its roads.[11] In 1904 the state legislature appropriated $2 million to improve roads when other states with similar programs spent less than one third that amount. Today, the metro area predominantly uses county bonds to maintain its road network and make improvements to its rail and bus service.

These public policies have helped Los Angeles, Santa Barbara, Madison, and Trenton achieve high index scores. These are by no means the only policies, however, that can improve how a community is built and the quality of life for the people who live there. For more ideas about local policy that can help your town grow in better ways visit www.smartgrowthamerica.org.

Conclusion

How we chose to build and develop affects everyone's day-to-day lives. How much we pay for housing and transportation, how long we spend commuting home, the economic opportunities in our communities, and even our personal health are all connected to how our neighborhoods and surrounding areas are built. These factors are better in compact, connected neighborhoods and worse in sprawling ones.

As residents and their elected leaders recognize the health, safety, and economic benefits of better development strategies, many chose to encourage this type of growth through changes to public regulations and incentives. Local elected officials, state leaders, and federal lawmakers can all help communities grow in ways that support these improved outcomes.

Smart Growth America helps communities understand the long-term impact of their development decisions. They work with public and private sectors so local communities can achieve multiple outcomes such as increased upward mobility and improved personal health. By providing this type of research, alongside policy ideas used in many of these communities, we hope more places will closely consider development decisions as key to long-term success.

This book provides an opportunity to reflect on many communities' successes, and to highlight the places where we, as a country, can do better. Visit www.smartgrowthamerica.org to learn more about our work and how your community can grow in better ways.

Case Examples for Planners

Notes

1 Learn more about the Los Angeles Transit Neighborhood Plans project at www.latnp.org/.
2 City of Los Angeles, CA (2008, February). Ordinance No. 179681. Available http://cityplanning.lacity.org/Code_Studies/Housing/DensityBonus.pdf.
3 City of Santa Barbara, CA Uses permitted in various zones. Available www.santabarbaraca.gov/civicax/filebank/blobdload.aspx?BlobID=17638.
4 City of Santa Barbara, CA (2011). Appendix C: History of the city. *General Plan Update.* Available www.santabarbaraca.gov/civicax/filebank/blobdload. aspx?BlobID=16916.
5 City of Santa Barbara, CA (2011). Land Use Element. Available www.santa barbaraca.gov/civicax/filebank/blobdload.aspx?BlobID=16898.
6 Learn more about the County of Santa Barbara, CA's Long Range Planning Division at http://longrange.sbcountyplanning.org/landuse_element.php.
7 Learn about all of Madison, WI's homebuyer assistance programs at www.cityofmadison.com/dpced/economicdevelopment/home-loans/228/.
8 Learn more about the Mansion Hill-James Madison Park Neighborhood Small Cap TIF Loan Program from the City of Madison's Economic Development Department. Available www.cityofmadison.com/dpced/economicdevelopment/mansion-hill-james-madison-park-neighborhood-small-cap-tif-loan-program/229/.
9 City of Madison, WI (2006, January). Appendix 4: City of Madison Strategic Management System Goals and Strategies re: Growth Management. *City of Madison Comprehensive Plan, Volume I.* Available www.cityofmadison. com/planning/ComprehensivePlan/dplan/v1/chapter5/v1c5.pdf.
10 For more information about Madison, WI's comprehensive plan see www.cityofmadison.com/planning/ComprehensivePlan/.
11 New Jersey Department of Transportation and Federal Highway Administration New Jersey Historic Preservation Office (2011, January). New Jersey Historic Roadway Study. Available www.state.nj.us/transportation/publicat/historicroadwaystudy.pdf.

References

Ewing, R., Pendall, R., and Chen, D. (2002). *Measuring Sprawl and its Impacts.* Smart Growth America, Washington, D.C.
Ewing, R., Pendall, R., and Chen, D. (2003a). Measuring sprawl and its transportation impacts. *Transportation Research Record*, 1832, 175–183.

Ewing R., Schmid, T., Killingsworth, R., Zlot, A., and Raudenbush, S. (2003b). Relationship between urban sprawl and physical activity, obesity, and morbidity. *American Journal of Health Promotion*, 18, 47–57.

Ewing, R., Schieber, R., and Zegeer, C. (2003c). Urban sprawl as a risk factor in motor vehicle occupant and pedestrian fatalities. *American Journal of Public Health*, 93, 1541–1545.

Index

Page numbers in *italics* denote an illustration, **bold** indicates a table, n indicates an endnote.

activity centering: D variable comparison 41; employment subcenters, impact of 27, 104; Madison's public policies 161–2; public health 78, 80; transportation outcomes 48, 49–50, 51, 53, 101–2, 154; urban centers 26, 92, 146; urbanized areas 156; variable loadings **27**, **95**, **149**; variables and their measurement 26–7, 92–3, 94, 146–7, 148

air pollution and sprawl 111–12

Air Quality Index (AQI) 112, 114

amenities, proximity to (walkscore) 25, 38n, 92, 128

American Community Survey (ACS) 42, 60, 112

Atlanta, GA 8, 97, **98**, *100*, 103, **151–2**

Behavioral Risk Factor Surveillance System (BRFSS) 74–5

Bischoff, Kendra 130

Brueckner, Jan 128

Center for Neighborhood Technology 119

Center for Transit Orientated Development 119

centering factor *see* activity centering

central business districts (CBDs): centering measurement 27, 92–3, 107n; identification methodology 26–7, 38n, 146–7

Cervero, Robert 41, 127–8

Charlotte, NC 157

Chetty, Raj 124–6, 129, 130

climatic factors: drive times 53; fatal crash rate 63–4; heating degree days and obesity 78; poor weather, less physicality 81; vehicle ownership 48; walk to work 49

commercial strip development 2–3, 56–7

compact development: BMI and obesity, relational factors 78; car dependency reduced 48, 101; compactness through densification 103; definition and related indicators 22; drive time reduction 53, 101, 154; D variables and travel behavior 41–2; employment subcenters and centering 104, *104*; fatal crash rate reduction 63, 64, 68; housing cost increases 121–2; life expectancy, causal pathways analyzed 116–17; physical activity, study findings 80–1; social capital 128; transit use increases 51,

Index

101, 154; transportation affordability 122–3; upward mobility opportunities 133–6; walking, positive relationship 49, 101, 128, 153–4

county sprawl indices, validation: analytical method 47; data and variables applied 42, **43**, 44–6, *44–6*; drive times 52–3, **54**; household vehicle ownership 47–8, **48**; relationship confirmations 53–4; transit mode shares 50–1, **52**; travel behavior 41–2; walk mode shares 49–50, **50**

crime: obesity rate rises 78; urban/rural safety, density related 111, 112–13; walking and safety fears 49

Cutsinger, Jackie 129

density as sprawl indicator 3, 6

Detroit 105, *105*

development density: density function 90–1, 107n; D variable comparison 41; Los Angeles's development policies 159–60; public health 78; transportation outcomes 48, 49, 51, 53, 101–2, 154; variable loadings **8**, **24**, **95**, 148, **149**; variables and their measurement 14–15, 23–4, 90–1, 145, 147–8

drive times: compactness and related reduction 53, 101, 154; county sprawl indices, validation 52–3, **54**; job-housing balance 127–8; metropolitan sprawl indices, validation 102

Dumbaugh, Eric 56–7

Duncan, Michael 127–8

D variables 41

education and income links: BMI and obesity 77, 78; chronic diseases 83; life expectancy rates 110; physical activity 80; upward mobility opportunities 130

employment density: calculations 38–9n; gross employment density 23; indications of sprawl 4

employment subcenters 27, 93, 104, *104*, 146–7

Environmental Protection Agency (EPA): Air Quality Index (AQI) 112, 114; sprawl research 1; VMT estimates 59

Equality of Opportunity Project 124–6, 130

ESRI Data & Maps 76

Ewing, Reid 5–6, 14, 57, 104–5

FBI uniform crime report 42, 112

four-or-more-way intersections 28, 94, 147

Freeman, Lance 128

Fulton, William 3–4, 103

Galster, George 129

gender, impact on variables: BMI and obesity 77; chronic diseases 83; physical activity 80; upward mobility 134–5; walk mode shares 49

Glaeser, Edward 4, 5

Goetz, Stephan 128

Gordon, Peter 105–6

Grant Parish, LA **31**, **35**, *37*

health outcomes and built environment study: BMI and obesity, relational factors 77–8, **79–80**; chronic diseases, relational factors **82–3**, 82–3; data sources and variables 74–6, **76–7**; geographic scale 73–4; physical activity engagement 78, 80–1, **81–2**; study limitations 84–5

Hickory, NC 97, **98**, *100*, **151–2**

Horner, Mark W. 127

household income: car ownership 47–8, 49, 63; drive times 52–3; fatal crash rate 63; housing and transport costs 123; housing expenditure 117–19, 121–2; income segregation and inequalities 129–30; job-housing balance 127–8; job inaccessibility 126–7; obesity rates 78; race and home ownership 129; transit use 51

Index

household size: large, facilitates car sharing 49, 50, 52; transport costs 122; vehicle miles traveled (VMT) 63; vehicle ownership, compact development 48, 101, 102

housing affordability: household expenditure 117–19; Housing+Transportation Affordability Index (H+T) 119; income segregation and inequalities 129–30; Madison's public policies 161; national indexes and standards 118–20

housing affordability and sprawl study: analytical method 120–1; data sources and variables 120, **121**; housing+transportation affordability 122–3, **123–4**; hypothesis 120; positive and negative variables 121–2, **123**

intersection density 28, 39n, 93–4, 147

Jackson County, KS 18, **19, 34**, *34*
Jargowsky, Paul A. 130
job-housing balance 127–8
job mix variable 25, 92, 145–6
job-population balance 24–5, 36–7n, 92, 145

Kahn, Matthew 129
Kain, John 126
Kockelman, Kara 41

land-use mix: D variable comparison 41; public health 80; Santa Barbara's public policies 160–1; transportation outcomes 53, 154; variable loadings **25, 95, 149**; variables and their measurement 24–6, 91–2, 104–5, 145–6
Largey, Ann 128
Las Vegas 3, 103
leapfrog development 2
Leyden, Kevin 128
life expectancy: compactness/sprawl indices 116–17, **117**; sociodemographic influences 109–10, 113; sprawl, causal

pathways analyzed 110–17, **114**, *115*, **116**
Li, Wenhao 56–7
Local Employment Dynamics (LED) 23, 90
Location Affordability Index (LAI) 119–20
Los Angeles: compactness ranking 106, 156; geographic size and sprawl perception 106–7, 150; policies assisting compact development 159–60; sprawl, early measurement 3, 4, 5, 6
low-density, single-use development 2, 3, 20, 33, **34**
Lund, Hollie 128

Madison, WI: activity centering policies 161–2
Margo, Robert 129
Mefford, Jessica 127
metropolitan sprawl indices, derivation and validation: boundary change impacts 105, *105*, *106*, 107; centering variables 92–3; compactness rankings, constants and movers 102–7, *104–6*; compactness/sprawl factors, variable loadings 94, **95–6**; development densities 90–1; index compilation and analysis 96–7, **98**, *99–100*; metropolitan areas/divisions, selection criteria 89–90; mixed-use variables 91–2; street accessibility 93–4; transportation outcomes analysis 97, 101–2, **101–3**
metropolitan statistical areas (MSAs): definition criteria 89–90, 107n; monocentric 27; polycentric 27, 104, *104*
mixed-use factor *see* land-use mix

National Association of Realtors 118
National Climatic Data Center 42, 60
National Land Cover Database (NLCD) 17
New Orleans 157
New York: compactness ranking 16, 32,

168

32–3, 97, *99*; housing affordability 122; metropolitan statistical areas (MSAs) 90

Nguyen, Mai 128

obesity: causes and risk factors 71, 110; sprawl correlations 72–3

Oil Price Information Service (OPIS) 42, 60

Olgethorpe County, GA 30–1, **31**, **35**, *36*

open space and activity level: accessibility and obesity 78; open space metric 75–6

Pendall, Rolf 3

Phoenix 3, 104–5, 150

Polk County, MN **19**, **34**, *35*

Portland 4, 6, 7, *106*, 107

public health: built environment impacts 72–3; health outcomes and built environment study 73–8, **76–7**, **79–80**, 80–5, **81–3**; obesity rises and activity declines 71

racial factors: BMI and obesity 77, 78; housing expenditure 121–2; income segregation 129–30; job inaccessibility 126–7; life expectancy 113; racial segregation 129; white population and travel behavior 47–8, 50, 62–3, 122

Reardon, Sean 130

refined county sprawl index: centering factor variables 26–7, **27**; compactness factors, correlation test 29, **29**; county-mix factor calculation 24–6, **25**; density variables (population and land cover) 23–4; four dimensions 23; index compilation and analysis 29–31, **30–1**; street accessibility variables 27–8; validity evaluation, 2000 & 2010 indices compared 31–3, *32–7*, **34–5**

Richardson, Harry 104–5

Rupasingha, Anil 128

San Francisco: compactness ranking 16, 97, *99*, 103, 151; housing affordability 122

Santa Barbara: land-use mix policies 160–1

Sarzynski, Andrea 128

satellite imagery applicability 4–5

single county sprawl index: county types 14; degree of change (2000-10) 19–20, *20–1*; density variables (population and land cover) 14–15; principal component analysis 15–16; ranking of counties 18, **19**; scale values 16; street accessibility variables 15; updated density variables 16–17, **18**

Smart Growth America (SGA) 1, 163

social capital 128

spatial mismatch hypothesis 126–7

sprawl *see* urban sprawl

Stockton, CA 157

street accessibility: public health 78; transportation outcomes 50, 51, 102, 154; Trenton's transportation plan 162–3; variable loadings **28**, **96**, **149**; variables and their measurement 15, 27–9, 93–4, 147

structural equation modeling (SEM) 60–1

traffic safety, sprawl/compactness study: casual path diagram 62, *63*; data sources 57, **58–9**; development pattern and crash rate 64–5, **65–8**, 68, 111; direct effects of variables 62–4, **64**; exogenous variables 59–60, **60**; results validation 62; retail sites and traffic incidents 56–7; structural equation modeling (SEM) 60–2; study limitations 68–9

transit mode shares: compactness, positive relationship 51, 101, 154; county sprawl indices, validation 50–1, **52**

travel behavior: built environment impacts 41–2; climatic factors 48, 49, 53, 63–4; fuel price 49, 51, 63; household vehicle ownership 47–8, **48**; transit mode shares 50–1; walking, factors influencing 49–50; young people's options 49, 50, 52

Index

Trenton, NJ: Transportation Master Plan 162–3

upward mobility: geographic factors and sprawl linkages 124–6; income segregation 129–30; job inaccessibility 126–8; low rates 123–4; racial segregation and housing 129; social capital 128

upward mobility and urban sprawl study: analytical method 132; data sources and variables 130–2, **131**; relationship findings and conformations 132–6, *133*, **134–5**

urbanized areas, longitudinal analysis: analysis compatibility 143; compactness/sprawl factors, variable loadings 148, **149**; compactness/sprawl indices 2000 & 2010 150–1, **151–2**; compactness/sprawl trends 156–7; definition and selection criteria 144; statistical methods 147–8; transportation outcomes, validation process 151–6, **153–5**; variables and their measurement 144–7

urban land area, data sources 15, 17

urban sprawl: air pollution, contribution to 111–12; built environment metrics **9**, 9–10, 41–2; crime rates, density related 112–13; definition and related indicators 2–3, 22; housing affordability, data sources 118–20; housing+transportation affordability study 120–3, **121**, **123–4**; job-housing imbalance 127–8; life expectancy, causal pathways 110–17, **114**, *115*;

measurement, early attempts 3–4, 6; multi-dimensional measures 5–6, 7; obesity, links to built environment 72; racial segregation and housing 129; retail sites and traffic incidents 56–7; social capital, mixed impact 128; traffic safety, sprawl/compactness study 57, **58–60**, 59–64, *63*, **65–8**, 68–9; upward mobility and social equality study 130–6, **131**, *133*, **134–5**; upward mobility and sprawl rankings 125–6

U.S. Department. Housing and Urban Development 118

vehicle miles traveled (VMT): compactness and crash reduction 64; compactness related reduction 63; development pattern and crash rate 56, 64–5, **65–8**, 68; fatal crash rate and variable relations 63–4; job-housing balance 127–8

walking: activity in compact areas 80; amenities and neighborhood ties 128; popular physical activity 71–2; positive and negative variables 49–50, 101–2, 153–4

walkscore 25, 38n, 92, 128

Washington D.C. 104, *104*

Wheeler, Christopher 130

white population (as variable): BMI and obesity rates 77; household vehicle ownership 47–8; housing expenditure 121–2; transit use 50, 122; vehicle miles traveled (VMT) 62–3

Whyte, William 89